A Baseline of Development

A Baseline of Development

Higher Education and Technology

Edited by Darrel W. Staat

ROWMAN & LITTLEFIELD
Lanham • Boulder • New York • London

Published by Rowman & Littlefield
An imprint of The Rowman & Littlefield Publishing Group, Inc.
4501 Forbes Boulevard, Suite 200, Lanham, Maryland 20706
www.rowman.com

6 Tinworth Street, London SE11 5AL

Copyright © 2019 by Darrel W. Staat

All rights reserved. No part of this book may be reproduced in any form or by any electronic or mechanical means, including information storage and retrieval systems, without written permission from the publisher, except by a reviewer who may quote passages in a review.

British Library Cataloguing in Publication Information Available

Library of Congress Cataloging-in-Publication Data

ISBN: 978-1-4758-5055-0 (cloth)
ISBN: 978-1-4758-5056-7 (pbk.)
ISBN: 978-1-4758-5057-4 (electronic)

Contents

Preface	vii
Acknowledgments	ix
Introduction	1
1 3D Printing: Additive Manufacturing *Sylvia Cox, Nita Johnson, and Melissa Price*	5
2 The Internet of Things *Sylvia Cox, Nita Johnson, and Melissa Price*	29
3 Autonomous Vehicles and Drones *Mark Roth and Renata Sims*	45
4 Personal Robots *Mark Roth and Renata Sims*	67
5 Human Genome *Ghada Gouda and Angelo Markantonakis*	81
6 Agricultural Genome *Ghada Gouda and Angelo Markantonakis*	97
7 Bitcoin/Blockchain *Darrel W. Staat*	115
8 Artificial Intelligence *Kira Ferris and Dahmon King*	125
9 Nanotechnology *Kira Ferris and Dahmon King*	137
10 Quantum Computing *Darrel W. Staat*	149

11 Future Technology Centers 157
Cameron Jackson and Don Miller

Epilogue 175

About the Editor 177

About the Contributors 179

Preface

Technologies of the twenty-first century already exist and are being developed. As educators we may be aware of some of them. We have seen robots in the movies. We have held 3D products in our hands and marveled at them. We have heard of Artificial Intelligence by way of Deep Blue, the computer that beat Garry Kasparov at chess some twenty years ago, or Watson, the computer that beat the two best players in the game of *Jeopardy* in 2011.

We may know that there is a luxury car called Tesla that actually can drive itself on the highway. We may have heard something about genome development. We sometimes see news reports on Bitcoin/blockchain. Most likely we have not paid too much attention to nanotechnology, or quantum computing.

These twenty-first-century technologies for the most part seem distant and blurred as we go about our daily work. They have not much direct impact on our jobs, families, and lives in general. It is easy not to think about them, let alone worry about them. They exist somewhere, but not in our backyards.

When I began my research to determine what was out there in the digital world and how it might impact education at the community college and university levels, my wife laughed and said I was talking about science fiction. Nothing to be concerned about. Her attitude has changed some. Maybe yours will, too, as you begin to see what is going on in higher education institutions across our country. Further, we when look around the world, we find that we are not developing these technologies on our own. Countries like China, North Korea, France, Germany, and England are moving ahead, some following us, others ahead of us.

This book is an initial attempt to determine what is currently going on with technologies in higher education in the United States. Our postsecondary institutions are moving ahead on a number of fronts, as is demonstrated by the research completed by the graduate students of Cohort 5 of the Ed.D. program entitled the Higher Education Executive Leadership at Wingate University in Wingate, North Carolina. The graduate students developed the research to support their interest in becoming knowledgeable community college leaders in the mid-twenty-first century. Their work can be of considerable interest and help to others leading institutions of higher education.

Acknowledgments

I would like to thank the nine graduate students of Cohort 5 and two from Cohort 6 who put in an untold number of hours researching and writing nine of the chapters in this book, which will be of practical use to current and future community college and university administrators.

I appreciate the support of my colleagues in the graduate education division at Wingate University who encouraged the writing of this book.

My thanks to Annette Digby, Ed.D., dean of the Thayer School of Education, who encouraged my efforts by her comments and leadership.

Finally, I appreciate the support of my wife, Beverly, who has had to adapt to being the wife of a professor who teaches, researches, and writes, after spending over twenty-three years as the wife of a community college and system president.

Introduction

Every day it becomes more obvious that the technologies of the twenty-first century are here to stay. As time passes, those technologies continue to develop, some out in the open and others behind the scenes. They are all developing in an exponential manner, which means that for a rather lengthy period of time, they develop in a linear manner, similar to technologies in the twentieth century. That is to say, they develop in a reasonable, predictable manner one step at a time. Then, seemingly out of nowhere, they develop exponentially at an explosive rate of speed.

TWENTIETH-CENTURY TECHNOLOGY

Take the development of the airplane as a twentieth-century technology. It begins with the Wright Brothers on a hill in North Carolina with a two-winged aircraft in 1903. Incremental improvements begin to take shape over the next few years. The decade of the 1920s arrives before a single-winged aircraft is successfully designed and flown. Approximately a decade later, single-engine fighter planes and four-engine bombers are developed and used in World War II. It is not until almost the end of the war that jet-propelled planes are developed. By the 1960s, jet-powered passenger planes are flying all over the United States and to Europe.

    Aircraft technology developed in an incremental, reasonable, predictable manner that could be easily seen and understood. Many other technologies developed in much the same way during the twentieth century—so much so that for the most part, as new technologies appeared on the scene, there was time to understand them and adapt to them. Everything from household appliances to automobiles were improved one step at a time, in a linear manner.

TWENTY-FIRST-CENTURY TECHNOLOGY

The products of the twenty-first century are another story. Most are connected to or result from the digital world. They are in some way connected to or driven by computer power and storage. The reason that makes a difference has to do with something called Moore's Law. Back in the 1960s, Gordon Moore, founder of Intel, made an observation that computer power appeared to be increasing at the rate of doubling every eighteen months because of the number of transistors that could be placed on a chip the size of a fingernail.

The doubling process of computer power and storage produced the ability of companies like Uber or Airbnb to go from an idea to a huge international business in a matter of a few years. All of the technologies discussed in this book, with the exception of quantum computing, are directly connected to or driven by increases in computer power and storage supported by Moore's Law.

If the Wright Brothers had produced their first aircraft in the year 2010 and could have taken advantage of Moore's Law, jet-propelled passenger planes might have been developed and flying internationally in less than a decade. By comparison, attempts were made to produce an operational robot in the early 1980s; however, since Moore's Law had not made a significant impact by that time, the robots could do little more than move around rather awkwardly.

PERSONAL ROBOTS

In 2005, the Japanese decided to solve a problem. Because of their extremely healthy diet, the Japanese tend to live longer. This created a problem for the small island country, as it did not have enough young people to provide the services needed to support its aging population. Consequently, the Japanese decided to develop a personal robot that could provide the basic services the aging population would need. In their first attempts, they produced small robots that could move with some elementary arm movements. If they had started in 1903, it would've taken them until the 1960s or '70s to develop a personal robot similar in looks and actions to a human being.

Thanks to Moore's Law, the increase in computer power and storage has allowed them to develop personal robots that both look human and can already provide some of the services needed by the aging population. Given another ten years, the personal robots produced in Japan will most likely take over a large percentage of the care given to the aging members of that society.

PURPOSE

The purpose of this book is to set a baseline of development in ten existing technologies of the twenty-first century. All of these technologies, with the exception of quantum computing, are using the computer power and storage forecasted by Moore's Law. This means that they will develop in what appears to be an apparent linear manner for some time, perhaps a number of years, before they reach a point where they expand phenomenally and rapidly, beyond any normal imaginings.

Why set that baseline? It is critical for educators and administrators in higher education to become actively aware of these ten existing technologies and the spawn that each of them may produce. That is to say, the technologies will have to be researched, watched, and planned for as they develop in an apparent linear manner, followed by a mind-bending exponential manner. It is that exponential development that may take those who are unaware by surprise.

BUSINESS AND TECHNOLOGY

Most participants in the world of business and industry are already aware of many, if not all, of the technologies discussed in this book. The leaders of those businesses and industries are looking to incorporate the benefits of these technologies as soon as possible. They understand that if they do not keep up with the bleeding edge of technological development, other companies or countries will, and that will put them at a distinct disadvantage. Falling behind the curve is to face bankruptcy, which no business wishes to encounter.

It is critical to understand that the technologies of the twenty-first century are here to stay. Although they may appear to be developing in a linear manner at present, it is important to know that they will soon develop in an exponential manner, at an exceedingly rapid velocity. Leaders and faculty in higher education need to be aware of what is out there in the digital world, find ways to keep up with the development of the technologies, and prepare to take action for the good of higher education institutions, students, and the community at large.

Chapter One

3D Printing

Additive Manufacturing

Sylvia Cox, Nita Johnson, and Melissa Price

It happens every day. A person has a problem and comes up with a great idea to solve it. Inspired by the amazing and yet often simple solution, the person dreams of creating the product and mass-producing it for the marketplace. Visions of presenting the product on the popular series *Shark Tank* (Lingner, 2018) vividly form in the inventor's mind.

And then, reality sets in as the person thinks it would be too difficult and costly to create a model to test the product. Sadly, the inventor's dream dies. Maybe that inventor did not know about additive manufacturing and cost-effective rapid prototyping readily available across the country in shops, both large and small.

Researchers and engineers began developing the 3D concept in the 1960s, but the first printers did not emerge until the 1980s. "Additive manufacturing first emerged in 1987 with stereolithography (SL) from 3D Systems, a process that solidifies thin layers of ultraviolet (UV) light-sensitive liquid polymer using a laser" (Wohlers & Gornet, 2014, p. 1). The birth of this new product and process method quietly began to change the way manufacturers and developers created and tested new products, and possibilities for creating with additive manufacturing continue to grow.

Additive manufacturing (AM) creates an object by adding materials, layer by layer, until the desired object is created. The traditional process for creating products is subtractive manufacturing. The subtractive process creates desired objects in the opposite way. Materials are subtracted from an object or metal until the desired object is created. This process is done by milling or turning the object (Gebhardt & Hotter, 2016). Once a successful mold is created, the subtractive process is an inexpensive process if the manufacturer is mass-producing a large quantity of items. However, the subtractive process produces excessive waste materials (M. Roth, personal communication, July 12, 2018).

AM technology produces a three-dimensional model or product from a mathematical model provided to the printer. The model is created with computer-aided design (CAD) technology. CAD information can be used, or it can be created by scanning an object (Chen, He, Yang, Niu, & Ren, 2017). A prototype is created with minimal costs, a significant advantage of AM, or 3-D printing. This rapid prototyping can happen in days. It allows inventors to adjust the product multiple times until the exact desired outcome is achieved.

AM technology combines materials science knowledge with laser and manufacturing technology to create functional prototypes as well as direct application parts. Over the past twenty years, AM technology has grown rapidly. There are names used for AM, such as rapid prototyping, solid free-form fabrication, and 3D printing, representing the different aspects of the technology.

> Compared with the conventional removing machining and distortion processing methods, AM technology of layer by layer processing has many prominent advantages, such as direct manufacturing process without molds, unrestricted to the degree of structural complexity, providing more freedom for the innovative design, high utilization of materials, and environment friendly. (Chen et al., 2017, p. 1)

AM technology has expanded into many industries and is now used for both commercial and personal applications. Three areas that have been significantly impacted by AM are the aerospace, medical, and construction industries. AM technology allows these industries to create lighter, more efficient products in minimal time (Chen et al., 2017).

The aerospace industry requires lightweight materials, and AM technology rapidly provides the industry with lightweight, specially designed parts. AM metal production is useful to the aerospace industry, and much research is being developed around improved and innovative uses for metal AM materials. In the past, the industry mainly used AM for testing products for fit and function, but now parts are produced as final parts, especially those parts made with metals. GE Airlines is now using AM metal technology to create fuel nozzles for airplane engines (Chen et al., 2017).

The medical field has greatly benefited from AM technology. Orthopedics, dentistry, plastic surgery, and regenerative medicine have all been impacted by the technology (Chen et al., 2017). In addition, 3D printing allows scans of patients to be used to assist doctors in preparing for surgery. These methods are beginning to show improvement in surgery outcomes when doctors prepare for surgery by using 3D printed materials (O. Harrysson, personal communication, June 14, 2018).

Implants and dentures are now commonly created with AM technology (Chen et al., 2017), with 3D bio-printing being the additive manufacturing of tissue and organs. This technology is at the cutting edge of regenerative medicine (Rayome, 2016). Bioengineering pioneer Dr. Anthony Atala, from the Wake Forest Institute for Regenerative Medicine (WFIRM), is part of the exciting discoveries taking place in the field today.

> This novel tissue and organ printer is an important advance in our quest to make replacement tissue for patients. It can fabricate stable, human-scale tissue of any shape. With further development, this technology could potentially be used to print living tissue and organ structures for surgical implementation. (Rayome, 2016, para. 16)

These and other new innovations in 3D bio-printing technology are rapidly advancing the field of medicine.

The construction industry is also utilizing AM to rapidly construct parts for buildings—as well as entire buildings. Architectural designs can be created using CAD and produced with AM technology. In 2014, ten buildings were constructed using 3D printing in twenty-four hours in China. The European aviation administration is currently testing the technology to determine whether buildings for a moon base can be created using AM (Chen et al., 2017).

ADDITIVE MANUFACTURING AND UNIVERSITIES

The explosion of additive manufacturing applications in business and industry has driven much of the research and curriculum development related to AM at universities. This sustained growth will continue to influence academia into the future.

> The rapid growth and disruptive potential of AM technologies demands education programs that address the fundamental principles of AM and likewise enable designers and engineers to realize its capabilities. Moreover, given the growing access to AM hardware, software, and materials, along with its hands-on nature, AM can be used as a teaching tool in several disciplines. (Go & Hart, 2016, p. 77)

Some universities have established research centers to explore innovations and research new uses and material development for AM technologies. In the United States, the National Additive Manufacturing Innovation Institute (NAMII), now America Makes, was created to research the possibilities and continue the development of AM. The Nanyang Technological University (NTU) Additive Manufacturing Center in Singapore was funded with advanced AM machines to foster the development of AM technology.

The Center for Innovative Materials Processing through Digital Deposition at Penn State University has many industry partners and works with government sponsors on research projects (Go & Hart, 2016). The website for Additive Manufacturing Today has created a directory of colleges and universities for high school students interested in attending a college or university with a robust 3D curriculum. Seventy-five colleges and universities with AM programs have been currently identified, and the number should continue to grow as the AM industry grows ("Additive manufacturing today," n.d.).

The curricula related to AM in universities includes topics in courses, entire courses, certificate programs, and degrees. AM innovation centers are often established at universities to enhance student learning and to provide a hub for innovation and research. These centers also serve as flagships for outreach events, conferences, and showcase centers to invite business and industry. These centers enhance universities' ability to provide students with opportunities to practically apply learning, test research hypotheses, and work with business/industry partners (Go & Hart, 2016).

AM has become firmly established in most engineering fields. Prototyping and CAD have become standard in most engineering programs. The availability of 3D printers has expanded beyond the engineering classroom doors to the library. The availability of 3D printers in libraries has expanded the technology access to most university students.

The general use of 3D printers at universities is not for research but to enhance learning and project development. Demonstrations and scale models can easily be made with 3D printers housed on university campuses, and these models can enhance learning in many fields (Van Epps, Huston, Sherrill, Alvar, & Bowen, 2015). These 3D-printed models can be extremely beneficial to students in a medical study. Anatomy and physiology can be studied without concern for the limited shelf life of formaldehyde-preserved animals and cadavers.

Cadavers begin to break down as soon as medical students begin the examination process, but 3D-printed materials provide exact replications of body parts and can be studied for an indefinite amount of time (O. Harrysson, personal communication, June 14, 2018). The possibilities for using 3D-printed materials are boundless and will provide opportunities for hands-on learning in many fields.

INDUSTRY, CERTIFICATES, AND UNIVERSITIES

Auburn University

AM has naturally found a home in mechanical engineering. Auburn University's mechanical engineering students have the opportunity to earn a fifteen-hour certificate in additive manufacturing ("Additive manufacturing," n.d.).

The development of the certificate program resulted as a response to an industry partnership. In June 2016, Auburn University was selected as one of eight universities worldwide to participate in the General Electric (GE) Additive Education Program.

The university developed the Center for Industrialized Additive Manufacturing in large part to respond to industry needs of GE's LEAP fuel nozzle production plant located near the university. GE business leaders' desire to have a trained workforce quickly meant the university had to respond differently.

Traditional curriculum development and slow approval processes for new programs would take too long to respond to the needs of GE. University materials professor Dr. Bart Prorok understood the need to respond quickly and began work to secure a $1.5 million grant from the National Institute of Standards and Technology (NIST). This grant would allow the university to research high-volume production of metal parts needed for innovation in GE's LEAP production.

The development of a certificate program in AM allowed the university to respond to GE's needs within a minimal time frame. Certificate programs do not require the same level of approvals as a four-year bachelor's program does and would allow students to begin enrolling in courses within a few years. Mechanical engineering students are able to earn the certificate by selecting AM certificate courses as free electives. Additionally, a degree in mechanical engineering is not required to enroll in the certificate program.

This allows other engineering and degree program students to earn the certificate in a similar manner as the mechanical engineering students. This allows Auburn the opportunity to meet the needs of industry while expanding AM education to the larger student population (Donaldson, 2018). Auburn's process is a good model for universities and colleges seeking to expand AM curricula.

Massachusetts Institute of Technology

The Massachusetts Institute of Technology (MIT) is addressing AM education in a variety of ways and is a leader in the development of AM education. MIT educates students on the mechanics of operating and maintenance of AM technology as well as teaching the underlining principles of the technology. These principles include machine design, materials processing, and manufacturing operations. MIT offers graduate level and advanced undergraduate level students in mechanical engineering fundamental applications of AM technology (Go & Hart, 2016).

The enthusiasm for learning about AM precipitated the development of a fourteen-week graduate level course. The course provides a multidisciplinary approach to educating students about AM and spurring the development of improvements in AM technology (Go & Hart, 2016). MIT developed an eleven-week online program for manufacturing professionals to increase knowledge of the fundamentals of AM. The lack of a broad understanding of AM has hindered the adoption of the technology. The course is designed to increase AM knowledge and to encourage the development and innovation of AM in organizations ("Additive manufacturing for innovative," n.d.).

ADAPT

The MIT Center for Additive and Digital Advanced Production Technologies (ADAPT) was created in 2017 to accelerate the use of AM and to explore innovations in AM ("MIT center for additive," n.d.). MIT is leading the way with innovations in AM technology. MIT engineers have developed a desktop 3D printer that is ten times faster than existing commercial printers (Chu, 2017).

CSAIL

MIT's Computer Science and Artificial Intelligence Laboratory (CSAIL) has designed a technique that will allow users to program all parts of a 3D-printed object to exact levels of stiffness and elasticity needed for the task. Printing softer and more elastic materials will make robots safer and will allow for more precise movements. The technology could be used to improve other materials as well, such as drones, phones, helmets, and shoes (Conner-Simmons, 2016).

Universities all over the country are researching the possibilities of additive manufacturing. These universities are creating innovative solutions for the aerospace, medical, construction, and manufacturing industries, as well as a host of other industries.

North Carolina State University

North Carolina State University (NC State) was established in 1887 as a land-grant college ("NC State's land grant," n.d.). In 1893, NC State graduated fourteen engineering students ("History," n.d.). NC State's commitment to innovation in engineering has been a cornerstone for the university since its foundation, and the Edward P. Fitts Department of Industrial and Systems Engineering (ISE) is leading the way in the advancement and research of AM.

CAMAL

The Center for Additive Manufacturing and Logistics (CAMAL) at North Carolina State University is a research and education center that provides educational and research opportunities for students in the study of additive manufacturing. The mission of the center is threefold. It seeks to provide the best university education possible, to provide research partners with an excellent environment for discovering and creating new knowledge in AM, and to provide clients and supporters with the best resources, publications, workshops, and projects ("Center for additive manufacturing," n.d.).

Dr. Ola Harrysson, Edward P. Fitts Distinguished Professor, is the co-director of CAMAL. Dr. Harrysson joined the faculty at North Carolina State in 2002. He teaches courses related to product development, manufacturing processes, additive manufacturing, and biomodeling. Dr. Harrysson's research focuses on AM production with a special emphasis on medical applications. His research on metal material uses in AM has provided insights and the development of innovated products and materials using AM ("Ola Harrysson," n.d.).

Dr. Harrysson has partnered with colleague Dr. Denis Marcellin-Little, an orthopedic surgeon at the North Carolina State College of Veterinary Medicine, to develop innovative implant solutions ("Ola Harrysson," n.d.). Dr. Harrysson has also worked with several medical doctors to develop innovations in medical implants. He has provided 3D scans to doctors for analysis prior to performing surgeries.

The practice of surgeons preparing for difficult surgeries using 3D models is more widely used in countries with government-provided national health care. Canada requires the process for some types of surgeries. However, American health-care companies have been hesitant to provide insurance coverage for such procedures. Dr. Harrysson and others are working to provide the data to American insurance companies proving that 3D models provide more successful surgical outcomes (O. Harrysson, personal communication, June 14, 2018).

Dr. Harrysson's experience and expertise serves him well as co-director of CAMAL. When Dr. Harrysson, a native of Sweden, arrived at the university, the ISE department only owned an old 3D wax printer. When he and a colleague attended the Solid Freeform Fabrication Symposium in 2003, he met a Swedish inventor for Arcam. The Swedish company had developed an electron-beam melting machine (EBM) for 3D printing. Dr. Harrysson believed this was the future of AM production, and he was right (O. Harrysson, personal communication, June 14, 2018).

The EBM uses electron beams to selectively melt layers of metal powder to build implants customized to the needs of individuals. The process allows for the fabrication of shapes and geometries that would otherwise be impossible to create with a 3D printer. The process allows implants to be created with such detail that it optimizes the development of the implant to address the specific needs of the individual, such as strength, bone ingrowth, soft tissue fixation, or reduction of stress shielding (NC State University, n.d.).

CAMAL facilities have a variety of advanced AM machines and supplementary equipment to produce and test innovations in AM. There are a variety of plastic-based AM machines such as stereolithography, fused deposition modeling, polyjet, ultrasonic consolidation, and powder consolidation. There are advanced CAD software programs that assist with the design of medical image reconstruction and implant design.

The facilities also house first-class manufacturing equipment such as CNC milling technology and CNC turning centers (North Carolina State University, n.d.). CAMAL received a Concept Laser M Cusing Lab, courtesy of the GE Additive Education Program. CAMAL developed AM curriculum for other institutions desiring to teach students about AM as a part of a NASA grant. The center hosted its third Additive Manufacturing Symposium, in April 2018. This event brought together experts in the field of AM in manufacturing, medicine, and other areas of academia to share current research and innovations in AM.

CAMAL is housed within the Edward P. Fitts Department of Industrial and Systems Engineering (ISE) at the university. Many AM innovation centers develop as a part of mechanical engineering programs, but CAMAL is an example of innovation in AM that has spread throughout different disciplines of engineering. Industrial engineering students at North Carolina State explore innovations in AM by partnering with other programs at the university and industry (O. Harrysson, personal communication, June 14, 2018).

North Carolina State's Industrial Engineering students learn by working with industry to solve real-world problems. The program integrates education and research related to the learning opportunities industry partners provide. Students learn all aspects of industrial systems to prepare for any industry.

BACHELOR'S DEGREES

The bachelor's degree program has specific courses to enhance AM learning. There is a foundations of design and 3D modeling course, a product development and rapid prototyping course, an introduction to computer-aided manufacturing course that teaches machine tooling with CAD and CNC equipment, and a variety of project-based courses that integrate the use of AM technologies ("Bachelor of science in," n.d.). There are also opportunities for AM learning at the graduate level (O. Harrysson, personal communication, June 14, 2018).

SUMMER CAMP

CAMAL provides the setting for hands-on learning and research development. ISE students learn about AM and share that knowledge with the community. The department hosts an annual summer camp for high school students that receives rave reviews from participants. The high school students enjoy the hands-on experiences of developing products using the equipment in CAMAL.

Dr. Harrysson is an AM ambassador and researcher. His enthusiasm for AM and his innovative research is advancing the field of AM. Dr. Harrysson works to educate his students, the community, academicians, and the industry about the benefits of AM and the unlimited possibilities for the future (O. Harrysson, personal communication, June 14, 2018).

ADDITIVE MANUFACTURING AND COMMUNITY COLLEGES

Community colleges were established to provide greater access to higher education for all Americans. The establishment was to provide a pathway to traditional liberal arts universities as a junior college, but the establishment also provided provision for comprehensive job training as well.

AACC

The American Association of Community Colleges (AACC) provides support for workforce and economic development divisions of community colleges. These divisions bring together community colleges, workforce boards, offices of economic development, and employers to improve the economic conditions of a community and to meet the needs of business and industry in the community. AACC provides assistance to colleges working with these partners to respond to regional labor market needs ("Workforce and economic development," n.d.).

Workforce and Community Development

The workforce and community development divisions of the colleges understand the role of working with business partners. Community colleges are providing short-term training for AM technologies. The AM training market is made up of a variety of options. Workshops and specific trainings for employees are provided through community colleges' continuing education departments. There are also a variety of AM courses available in technical curriculum programs at community colleges (Thurn, Balc, Gebhardt, & Kessler, 2017).

Achieving the Dream

Organizations are supporting community colleges in the development of AM programs, and AM courses or certificates are usually taught within the programs. Achieving the Dream began the Community College Advanced Manufacturing Career Pathways Initiative to close skills gaps in AM careers for community college students. The program is funded by the Arconic Foundation, and three community colleges are a part of the program: Cuyahoga Community College, Muskegon Community College, and Westmoreland County Community College ("Achieving the dream," n.d.).

Cuyahoga Community College

Cuyahoga Community College provides students with an opportunity to earn a 3D Digital Design and Manufacturing Technology certificate. The thirty-five-hour program provides students with a comprehensive overview of AM and skills necessary in advanced manufacturing AM production ("3D digital design and," n.d.). Cuyahoga Community College also partners with America Makes and contributed to the 2016 Additive Manufacturing Body of Knowledge Update provided by Additive Manufacturing Leadership Initiative ("2016 additive manufacturing body," n.d.).

Muskegon Community College's Applied Technology Department houses an AM lab. Westmoreland County Community College has an Advanced Technology Center that provides AM training for students in advanced technology programs ("Advanced technology center," n.d.).

GE Additive Education Program

Community colleges aligned with industry partners are making advances in workforce and technical training in AM. The GE Additive Education Program supports colleges and universities in the advancement of additive education. Universities usually receive a large majority of these awards, but a few community colleges are being recognized and awarded through GE.

Calhoun Community College

Calhoun Community College was selected as one of five colleges and universities and the only community college to receive the GE Additive Education Program for the 2018–2019 cycle from among five hundred colleges and universities worldwide. The program provides a Concept Laser Mlab 200R machine to the college. The direct metal laser melting (DMLM) AM system is worth more than $1.25 million. It uses lasers to melt layers of fine metal powder and create complex geometries directly from a CAD file ("Calhoun among five colleges," 2018).

Calhoun Community College provides a short-term certificate program in additive manufacturing design technology. These courses are also a part of the Design Drafting Technology AAS degree program ("Advanced manufacturing AAS degree," n.d.). Community colleges are providing certificate programs similar to some universities to meet the immediate demands of the industry while providing the courses as electives to two-year degree programs.

America Makes and the National Science Foundation

Organizations like America Makes and the National Science Foundation are also impacting the education and curricula development of programs at community colleges. These organizations foster the growth of innovation in AM at community colleges. America Makes is partnering with Lightweight Innovations for Tomorrow (LIFT), the National Additive Manufacturing Innovation Institute, and Cincinnati State Technical and Community College (CSTCC) to develop open resource curriculum for workers and students.

SKILLS GAP

There is a skills gap in the workforce, technology advances in AM are moving quickly, and the growth of AM is exponential in the manufacturing industry. These partners realize the need to provide up-to-date materials to community colleges and other workforce trainers in order to make sure that America remains a leader in AM production and technology ("America makes and LIFT," 2017).

The National Science Foundation (NSF) provides grant opportunities for a wide variety of AM outreach, research, and educational opportunities. The Advance Technological Education (ATE) program focuses primarily on two-year institutions in higher education in the education of technicians for high-technology fields. The program supports curriculum development and professional development for college faculty and secondary schoolteachers ("Advanced technological manufacturing," n.d.). NSF provides funds to allow community colleges to develop additive manufacturing curricula.

Somerset Community College

Somerset Community College (SCC) in Somerset, Kentucky, was awarded an Advanced Technology Education Program award from NSF. The project, Additive Manufacturing: Expanding Futures in Appalachia, is designed to stimulate growth in AM and employability skills of technician graduates of SCC. The program provides development for entrepreneurs utilizing additive manufacturing.

The program brings awareness of AM to SCC faculty, staff, and students, as well as community members and K–12 stakeholders. The project will serve as a model for other community colleges seeking to develop an accredited AM certificate program ("Additive manufacturing: expanding futures," n.d.).

Eric Woolridge is a professor of mechanical engineering at SCC and program lead for the NSF grant. His background as an architect and mechanical engineer brings invaluable knowledge to his current role. The skills Woolridge has developed from the fields of engineering and architecture have allowed him to design innovative curricula and practical lessons for students at SCC. Woolridge also provided AM educational outreach events to the community, other colleges, organizations, businesses, and industry.

Digital Printing Technology

Woolridge designed a Digital Printing Technology (3D) certificate for students at SCC. The program addresses AM technology as well as business and entrepreneur education for the student who would like to start a business. Some courses in the certificate program can be used to meet a statewide digital literacy requirement for any student at SCC, and other courses can be used as electives for other degree programs at SCC (E. Woolridge, personal communication, July 10, 2018).

The Digital Printing Technology (3D) certificate teaches students the AM technology and skills needed, but it also teaches the students entrepreneurial skills. "Students have good ideas, but they don't know how to market their products" (E. Woolridge, personal communication, July 10, 2018). The rapid prototyping provided by 3D printers allows anyone to be an inventor. There are uses for AM technology in every industry, such as cosmetology, gaming design, and the service parts and repair industry.

The possibilities are endless with AM. Hearing aids, dental work, and even tennis shoes are all printed using AM technology, and Woolridge's students learn about all the innovations and applications of AM. CAD design and digital scanning allow for innovation with simple 3D printers (E. Woolridge, personal communication, July 10, 2018).

Test Case Studies

Woolridge and students test case studies related to AM technology. One such case study involved creating a test product for a cosmetology invention. A cosmetologist had an idea for creating a tool that could dry hair through a suction and humidity reduction process. This type of process would allow quick drying of hair without the damage associated with heat drying. The prototype was created with inexpensive 3D printers.

Although there are still concerns with the tool, the inventor feels confident enough to pursue a patent for the product (E. Woolridge, personal communication, July 10, 2018). This case study and others conducted by Woolridge and students at SCC educate the community and inform businesses and industry on the potential for AM uses in the area. Students learn that the potential of AM can sometimes be delivered in a small package.

Students in the program are invited to take home inexpensive 3D printers. The printers cost approximately two hundred dollars. After six months the students are asked to return the printers. All of the students who have experienced having a 3D printer at home have eventually purchased a similar product. Once students learn the possibilities of 3D printing, they find it difficult to live without one.

The Future of 3D Printing

In the near future, Woolridge believes 3D printers will become like personal computers and most every home will own one (E. Woolridge, personal communication, July 10, 2018). Woolridge believes the AM industry is getting ready to explode. Industries, individuals, and colleges currently ignoring AM will quickly fall behind in this technology. The startup cost for developing AM certificates at community colleges are minimal and are well worth the investment, according to Woolridge.

"Ignore this technology at your own risk. I agree with GE, you're either going to be the leader in additive or a victim of it" (E. Woolridge, personal communication, July 10, 2018). SCC is a great example of a community college utilizing resources effectively to maximize benefits to students. SCC is educating students and the community about the economic advantages and scope of AM both now and in the future.

FLORENCE-DARLINGTON TECHNICAL COLLEGE

Florence-Darlington Technical College (FDTC) in Florence, South Carolina, is the home of Southeastern Institute of Manufacturing and Technology (SiMT). The partnership between the SiMT and FDTC curriculum program has created an opportunity for students to learn AM and for the SiMT to provide AM services to the community. The SiMT has the largest 3D plastic and metal prototyping tools available in the Southeast ("Additive manufacturing: 3D printing," n.d.).

Certificate Levels

The variety of metal and plastics production at the community college allows students to be trained on the properties of different materials. Three AM certificates are available through FDTC. Additive Manufacturing Designer Level I, Additive Manufacturing Technician Level II, and Rapid Prototyping Lab Technician are available certificates and can be completed in two semesters. These courses can also be used as electives in FDTC's mechanical engineering program, but the skills in the certificates allow students to gain employment in the AM field.

"The technology is so new that companies are calling all the time trying to steal our instructors" (M. Roth, personal communication, July 12, 2018). Mark Roth is the vice president of the SiMT and sees AM technology as a growing field. The SiMT provides opportunities to teach technicians while at the same time serving the community, state, country, and other nations with AM technology.

Services

AM at the SiMT provides services to forty states and eight countries. Rapid prototyping serves businesses and inventors. "The biggest benefit of AM is being able to get your product developed faster. You can take a concept, get it printed, and actually have a working model within two days" (J. Melton, personal communication, July 12, 2018). The SiMT has worked with several inventors to produce prototypes.

One such prototype was a sample stick to collect saliva from dogs to determine if the dogs had diabetes. The sample stick was small and took several variations to develop the final stick, but the results are a product that is uniquely designed for the job. The relatively inexpensive and quick process allowed the inventor to produce a stick that would be the most efficient for collecting samples (J. Melton, personal communication, July 12, 2018).

Variety of 3D Printing

The SiMT is home to eight different 3D printers. The printers produce small prototypes for inventors and larger projects for industry. The SiMT has an EOS M290. This machine uses metals such as stainless steel and titanium to produce products. AM metal production can take a variety of metal composites to create a product. In traditional production, metals often do not blend with ease, but AM allows metal production with a variety of metals to make products with intricate details (M. Roth, personal communication, July 12, 2018).

The institute has produced parts for race car drivers and has done some mass production for boats. The possibilities for development are endless, and the industry continues to grow (J. Melton, personal communication, July 12, 2018). FDTC also has the Gould Business Incubator. The incubator houses the SiMT MakerSpace. This business provides membership to a space that has twelve 3D printers.

The printers can be used to create fun or useful projects. These small 3D printers are introducing the FDTC community to the possibilities of 3D printing. The concepts of AM can be taught on a small machine. Community colleges that would like to start an AM program can begin with simple 3D printers and a CAD design course.

The overhead to start a program is low, and there are enough models for certificate programs throughout the country that community colleges should invest in this technology. The industry has not peaked. "It is like an upside-down funnel and we are just at the top of the funnel. There is still a great deal of growth to happen in this industry" (M. Roth, personal communication, July 12, 2018).

SHORT TERM (1–5 YEARS)

In the next three to five years, the impacts of Additive Manufacturing ambassadors will expand the general knowledge about the technology. Community college AM ambassadors, such as Eric Woolridge at SCC, and Mark Roth and Jonathan Melton at the SiMT, share the importance of learning about AM. Dr. John Hart, a professor at MIT, promotes the importance of introducing 3D printing as a part of children's early education. Hart also teaches a graduate course in AM that is bringing awareness to the technology (Chu, 2016). AM ambassadors are passionate about the possibilities of AM and want the technology to be a part of everyday life.

There is a shortage of industry technicians with AM knowledge. Community colleges in the short term need to prepare workforce training for the immediate needs of employers while still developing more skilled AM technicians in traditional technical curriculum programs. Community colleges also need to prepare students to be AM entrepreneurs. The relatively low cost of 3D printers will continue to decrease, and 3D printers will be affordable for startup entrepreneurs (E. Woolridge, personal communication, July 10, 2018).

> There are very, very few machine operators out there because there are not that many systems around. So, when a company buys a 3D printer, then they start looking to see who else has 3D printers. And they try to hire their people away from them. What really needs to happen is that the community colleges need to get into this and train the operators. (O. Harrysson, personal communication, June 14, 2018)

CNC operators will be needed to process metal additives finishing as well as 3D printing operators, and there are not enough operators in the field (O. Harrysson, personal communication, June 14, 2018). As baby boomers retire, the shortage of workers will get worse, and many of the current operators do not have children who will take over for them. This is going to create a shortage that community colleges need to be prepared to fill with an educated workforce (J. Melton, personal communication, July 12, 2018).

Rapid prototyping with AM will replace traditional subtractive methods. "As capabilities to 3D print in color, in multiple materials, and in metals continue to improve, so the range and quality of products and components that can be rapidly prototyped continues to expand" (Barnatt, 2016, p. 7). Research in metals and other materials will increase the opportunities for printing with different materials, and rapid prototyping will be expanded into different areas because of material uses and capabilities (Dr. O. Harrysson, personal communication, June 14, 2018).

Direct digital manufacturing (DDM) is being used. This process prints directly from a CAD file and allows the information to be sent to a 3D printer anywhere. This method has potential to grow in the short term. Customization and personalization of products will be more common and will allow customers to create a product that is unique (Barnatt, 2016, p. 7).

BMW already allows for the customization of cars that are 3D-printed, and tennis shoes are being created for athletes. The customization is for people who consider money to be no object (Dr. O. Harrysson, personal communication, June 14, 2018). In the near future, customization will be more affordable and more prevalent. Bigger companies such as GE and Hewlett-Packard are expanding AM use within their companies, and this will increase the demand for works in the field.

GE Additive is pushing for universities and colleges to increase education to assist in providing a trained workforce. The demands of industry will increase the need for community colleges and universities to prepare students to work in the field of AM in a variety of roles (Dr. O. Harrysson, personal communication, June 14, 2018).

MID-TERM (5–10 YEARS)

In the next five to ten years, colleges and universities will need to take an interdisciplinary approach to the teaching of AM. Material processing and material sciences will need to be developed together.

> The materials research approach, which brings together researchers from across different science and engineering fields to solve complex problems, provides a model for solving 21st century challenges in energy, environment and sustainability; health care and medicine; vulnerability to human and natural threats; and expanding and enhancing human capability and joy (Paiste, 2017, para. 8).

Many new technologies will depend upon each other, and specialization will need to be balanced with a multifaceted technician. Students will need to be prepared to think critically and address a variety of problems in the industry. Specialized customization of parts will become commonplace.

Massive storage buildings that house thousands of parts for repair will begin to disappear and will be replaced with 3D-printed parts-on-demand or printing in small quantities. This will greatly reduce costs for the industry (O. Harrysson, personal communication, June 14, 2018). Technicians who can use 3D printing and understand the art of orientation of a printed product will be in great demand (M. Roth, personal communication, July 12, 2018).

Workforce employees will still be needed, and jobs will not disappear. AM jobs will just require a different and more complex skill set. As a result, the educational system needs to prepare workers with different skill sets than today (O. Harrysson, personal communication, June 14, 2018). AM printer technology will change, and more hybrid systems will exist.

The combination of subtractive and additive processes is being developed in a process called digital additive subtractive hybrid manufacturing (DASH). This system integrates advanced metal additive and subtractive manufacturing processes into a manufacturing tool that creates a finished product (Basinger et al., 2018).

Advances in 3D printing will allow for increased production of buildings and construction using 3D-printed concrete. This material provides design freedom, is low cost, and does not require as many traditional labors to produce (Panda, Tay, Paul, & Tan, 2018).

Students at MIT are researching the possibilities of printing food. 3D-printed foods could be packed flat to ship, which could significantly reduce shipping costs. The transformation for packaging and eating foods could be changed with 3D printing (Clark, 2017). Vitamins could be provided in the food to increase the nutritional value, and people with specific dietary needs could bring 3D-printed food along when traveling (O. Harrysson, personal communication, June 14, 2018).

Cake decorations created through 3D printing are already in stores, and the possibilities for other food uses could change the way we eat (M. Roth, personal communication, July 12, 2018). In the next five to ten years, AM will produce many consumers' products, and AM plants will begin to replace some traditional manufacturing plants. AM technology is already beginning to create mass production of some smaller objects. As 3D-machines improve and materials science increases, mass production using AM will be a part of the manufacturing sector (O. Harrysson, personal communication, June 14, 2018).

LONG TERM (10–20 YEARS)

In the next ten to twenty years, AM production will become a part of many processes. Micro-nano 3D printing may provide a way to create an alternative way to create conductive materials in an efficient and cost-effective way. These materials exhibit excellent electrical conductivity, and 3D micro-nano printing could produce micro-batteries that could increase energy density.

"Smart materials are defined as stimulus-responsive materials that change their shape or functional properties under certain stimuli such as temperature, solvent, pH, electricity, light, and so on" (Chang et al., 2018, p. 10).

In addition, 3D bio-printing has the potential to revolutionize the medical industry and the way that health care is delivered to patients. Researchers at the University of Toronto have developed a means of 3D bio-printing skin to provide skin grafts for burn patients (Shaddock, 2018). Combining AM with smart materials may create a product that is being referred to as 4D printing. This technology offers the possibility of creating shape-shifting materials, and 4D printing that can shape-shift could make it possible to control biomedical processes or drug delivery.

These 4D-printed smart materials can be developed into complex structures that have a specific responsiveness depending upon the situation and conditions. "As high-resolution 4D printing techniques rapidly evolve, micro/nano-scale stimuli-responsive architecture together with multiscale design, multi-material print, and time-dependent function regulation will definitely find wide application in various fields" (Chang et al., 2018, p. 15).

The medical, manufacturing, and building fields will have multiple uses for AM and AM technologies. Customization for orthopedic processes will improve, and surgeons will commonly use 3D models. 3D printing will be a natural part of our everyday lives (O. Harrysson, personal communication, June 14, 2018).

ADVICE FOR HIGHER EDUCATION ADMINISTRATORS

AM technology continues to grow. The industry is still developing, and with the increase in material possibilities there is still great opportunity for growth in the future. Community colleges need to invest in AM technologies and prepare students for jobs in AM. The industry is in need of workers, and community colleges must be prepared to meet the demands of industry. The 3D machines can be used to teach the additive processes and to prepare students to work in the industry.

This technology, unlike many other future technologies, is affordable for colleges and provides wonderful opportunities for students with little capital investment (M. Roth, personal communication, July 12, 2018). Ignoring this technology means that community colleges will become victims of the technology. The manufacturing industry and many small businesses will expect students to understand how to use 3D technology, and students who do not have AM knowledge will not be as competitive in the job market (E. Woolridge, personal communication, July 10, 2018).

> The rapid growth and disruptive potential of AM technologies demands education programs that address the fundamental principles of AM and likewise enable designers and engineers to realize its capabilities. Moreover, given the growing access to AM hardware, software, and materials, along with its hands-on nature, AM can be used as a teaching tool in several disciplines. (Go & Hart, 2016, p. 77)

Community college administrators cannot afford to ignore the exponential growth of AM and the varied possibilities for the future. Partnerships abound in this time of AM ambassadors and awareness. It is a wonderful time for community colleges to partner with industry and universities. Community colleges can provide much-needed research information to universities, and universities can expand opportunities for community colleges.

Community college students will want to transfer to universities. Building pathways from community colleges to universities in the field of AM is an important opportunity for community college students and industry partners who need a workforce of employees educated at various levels. Achieving the Dream, America Makes, the National Science Foundation, and many other organizations provide educational opportunities and grant funding for colleges in the field of AM.

Skills USA is a partnership of students, teachers, and industry partners working to prepare a trained workforce. Competitions in various fields help students with learning in different fields. The AM Skills USA contest prepares students and challenges students to understand the technology and utilize it in innovated ways ("SkillsUSA additive manufacturing contest," n.d.).

These contests can enhance the skills of students related to AM and foster growth and development among students. Community college administrators should invest in creating a local chapter of Skills USA and should provide students with the opportunity to compete in local, regional, state, and national competitions.

ADVICE FOR STUDENTS

Students should embrace every opportunity to learn about AM technology. If possible, purchasing a 3D printer for home use can provide opportunities to explore the many uses of AM. Internships and work experience in AM fields can be extremely valuable. Experience with the technology helps knowledge turn into expertise in the field.

CONCLUSION

The job outlook for technicians in the field of AM is great (J. Melton, personal communication, July 12, 2018). The AM field will continue to grow in the future, and the hands-on approach in this field makes learning fun. New innovations for AM in the future will be exponential.

CHAPTER SUMMARY

- The birth of 3D printing, additive manufacturing, quietly began to change the way manufacturers and developers created and tested new product possibilities.
- Additive manufacturing combines materials science knowledge with laser and manufacturing technology to create functional prototypes as well as direct application parts.
- This 3D technology is at the cutting edge of regenerative medicine.
- In 2014, ten buildings were constructed in twenty-four hours in China using 3D printing.
- In the United States, the National Additive Manufacturing Innovation Institute was created to research possibilities and continue the development of additive manufacturing.
- The curricula related to additive manufacturing in universities includes 3D-printing topics in courses, entire courses, certificate programs, and degrees.
- New 3D-printed models can be extremely beneficial to students in medical study.
- Anatomy and physiology can be studied without concern for the limited shelf life of formaldehyde-preserved animals and cadavers.
- Auburn University's mechanical engineering students have the opportunity to earn a fifteen-hour certificate in additive manufacturing.
- The Massachusetts Institute of Technology educates students on the mechanics of operating and maintaining additive manufacturing technology as well as teaching the underlying principles of the technology.
- MIT's computer science and artificial intelligence laboratory has designed a technique that will allow users to program all parts of a 3D-printed object to the exact levels of stiffness and elasticity needed for the task.
- The Center for Additive Manufacturing and Logistics at North Carolina State University is a research and education center that provides educational and research opportunities for students in the study of additive manufacturing.
- A Swedish company developed an electron beam melting machine for 3-D printing. The machine uses electron beams to selectively melt layers of metal powder to build implants customized to the needs of individuals.
- North Carolina State University's industrial engineering students learn by working with the industry to solve real-world problems. The program

- integrates education and research related to the learning opportunities industry partners provide.
- Workshops in specific training for employees are provided through community colleges' continuing education department in the area of additive manufacturing.
- Cuyahoga Community College provides students with an opportunity to earn a 3D digital design and manufacturing technology certificate.
- Organizations like America Makes and the National Science Foundation are also impacting education in the curricula development of additive manufacturing programs at community colleges.
- Somerset Community College in Kentucky was awarded an advanced technology education program from the National Science Foundation on additive manufacturing.
- Hearing aids, dental work, and even tennis shoes are all printed using additive manufacturing technology.
- The startup cost for developing additive manufacturing certificates at community colleges are minimal and well worth the investment.
- Three additive manufacturing certificates are available through Florence-Darlington Technical College: Additive Manufacturing Designer Level I, Additive Manufacturing Technician Level II, and Rapid Prototyping Lab Technician.
- There is a shortage of industry technicians with additive manufacturing knowledge.
- Direct digital manufacturing is being used and will continue to grow. This process prints directly from a CAD file and allows the information to be sent to a 3D printer anywhere.
- In the next five to ten years, colleges and universities will need to take an interdisciplinary approach to the teaching of additive manufacturing.
- Massive storage buildings that house thousands of parts for repair will begin to disappear and will be replaced with 3D-printed parts-on-demand or printing in small quantities.
- Students at MIT are researching the possibilities of printing food, which could be packed flat to ship and significantly reduce shipping costs.
- 3D bio-printing has the potential to revolutionize the medical industry and how health care is delivered to patients.
- Community colleges need to invest in additive manufacturing technologies and prepare students for jobs in that field.
- Students should embrace every opportunity to learn about additive manufacturing. If possible, purchasing a 3D printer for home use could provide opportunities to explore the many uses of additive manufacturing.
- The job outlook for technicians in the field of additive manufacturing is great.

REFERENCES

Achieving the dream. (n.d.). Retrieved on June 28, 2018, from http://www.achievingthedream.org/resources/initiatives/community-college-advanced-manufacturing-career-pathways.
Additive manufacturing. (n.d.). Retrieved on July 15, 2018, from https://www.additivemanufacturing.media/.
Additive Manufacturing: Expanding Futures in Appalachia. (n.d.). Retrieved on June 28, 2018, from https://www.nsf.gov/awardsearch/showAward?AWD_ID=1600081.
Additive manufacturing for innovative design and production. (n.d.). Retrieved on July 17, 2018 from https://additivemanufacturing.mit.edu/?gclid=EAIaIQobChMI4-rK3q6z3AIVDYnICh2JnAC-EAAYASAAEgJ1jfD_BwE.
Additive manufacturing today. (n.d.). Retrieved on July 7, 2018, from https://additivemanufacturingtoday.com.
Additive manufacturing: 3D printing. (n.d.). Retrieved on June 28, 2018, from http://simt.com/cgi-bin/p/awtp-custom.cgi?d=simt&page=27175.
Advanced manufacturing AAS degree. (n.d.). Retrieved on June 28, 2018, from http://webnt.calhoun.edu/curriculumcard/Design-Drafting.pdf.
Advanced technological manufacturing. (n.d.). Retrieved on June 28, 2018, from https://www.nsf.gov/funding/pgm_summ.jsp?pims_id=5464.
Advanced technology center. (n.d.). Retrieved on June 28, 2018, from https://www.co.westmoreland.pa.us/2160/Advanced-Technology-Center.
America Makes and LIFT join with Cincinnati State to create lightweight additive manufacturing curriculum. (2017, March 1). Retrieved from https://www.americamakes.us/americamakes-lift-join-cincinnati-state-create-lightweight-additive-manufacturing-curriculum/.
Bachelor of science in industrial engineering. (n.d.). Retrieved on July 2, 2018, from https://www.ise.ncsu.edu/current-students/curriculum/.
Barnatt, C. (2016). *3D printing* (3rd ed.). Printed and bound on demand.
Basinger, K. L., Keough, C. B., Webster, C. E., Wysk, R. A., Martin, T. M., & Harrysson, O. L. (2018). Development of a modular computer-hybrid manufacturing of pockets, holes, and flat surfaces. *The International Journal of Advanced Manufacturing Technology, 96*, 2407–20. https://doi.org/10.1007/s00170-018-1674-x.
Calhoun among five colleges and universities worldwide selected to receive additive manufacturing equipment from GE additive. (2018, June 25). Retrieved from https://calhoun.edu/calhoun-among-five-colleges-and-universities-worldwide-selected-to-receive-additive-manufacturing-equipment-from-ge-additive/.
Center for additive manufacturing and logistics. (n.d.). Retrieved on July 2, 2018, from https://camal.ncsu.edu/about-us-2/mission/.
Chang, J., He, J., Mao, M., Zhou, W., Lei, Q., Li, X., Li, D., Chua, C., & Zhao, X. (2018). Advanced material strategies for next-generation additive manufacturing. *Materials, 11*(166), 1–19. doi:10.3390/ma11010166.
Chen, L., He, Y., Yang, Y., Niu, S., & Ren, H. (2017). The research status and development trend of additive manufacturing technology. *International Journal of Advanced Manufacturing Technology, 89*(9–12), 3651–60. https://doi.org/10.1007/s00170-016-9335-4.
Chu, J. (2017, November 29). New 3-D printer is 10 times faster than commercial counterparts: New design may open new opportunities for 3-D-printing technology. *MIT news*. Retrieved from http://news.mit.edu/2017/new-3-d-printer-10-times-faster-commercial-counterparts-1129.
Chu, J. (2016, May 11). 3-D printing 101: As MIT course challenges students to reinvent 3-D printing, professor aims to share approach with others. *MIT News*. Retrieved from http://news.mit.edu/2016/mit-course-3-d-printing-101-0511.
Clark, N. (2017, July 20). Shape-shifting 3d-printed food may soup up industry, *The Chemical Engineer*. Retrieved from https://www.thechemicalengineer.com/features/snapshot-shape-shifting-3d-printed-food-91314/.
Conner-Simmons, A. (2016, October 3). 3-D-printed robots with shock-absorbing skins: By "programming" customized soft materials, CSAIL team can 3-D print safer, nimbler, more

durable robots. *MIT news*. Retrieved from http://news.mit.edu/2016/3-d-printed-robots-shock-absorbing-skins-1003.
Donaldson, B. (2018, April 4). Auburn's roadmap to additive manufacturing education. Retrieved from https://www.additivemanufacturing.media/articles/auburn-universitys-roadmap-to-additive-manufacturing-education.
Gebhardt, A., & Hotter, J. (2016). *Additive manufacturing: 3D printing for prototyping and manufacturing*. Cincinnati, OH: Hanser.
Go, J., & Hart, A. J. (2016). A framework for teaching the fundamentals of additive manufacturing and enabling rapid innovation. *Additive Manufacturing, 10*, 76–87. https://doi.org/10.1016/j.addma.2016.03.001.
History. (n.d.). Retrieved on July 2, 2018, from https://www.engr.ncsu.edu/about/history/.
Lingner, Y. (Executive Producer). (2018). *Shark Tank* [Television series]. Hollywood, CA: American Broadcasting Company.
MIT center for additive and digital advanced production technologies. (n.d.). Retrieved on July 17, 2018, from http://adapt.mit.edu/.
NC State's land grant. (n.d.). Retrieved on July 2, 2018, from https://historicalstate.lib.ncsu.edu/timelines/nc-state-s-land-grant.
NC State University. (n.d.). *Additive manufacturing at NC State: Biomedical research*. [Pamphlet]. Raleigh, NC.
Ola Harrysson. (n.d.). Retrieved on July 2, 2018, from https://www.ise.ncsu.edu/people/oaharrys/.
Paiste, D. (2017, November 5). Interdisciplinary materials science a key to progress: Bringing together researchers from different science and engineering fields for materials day symposium promises solutions to energy, health, and other needs. *MIT News*. Retrieved from http://news.mit.edu/2017/mit-materials-day-symposium-1106.
Panda, B., Tay, Y. W. D., Paul, S. C., & Tan, M. J. (2018). Current challenges and future potential of 3D concrete printing. *Materialwissenschaft und Werkstofftechnik, 49*(5), 666–73. doi: 10.1002/mawe.201700279.
Rayome, A. D. (2016, August 12). How 4 universities are using 3D printing to create ears, cartilage and blood cells. *TechRepublic*. Retrieved from https://www.techrepublic.com/article/how-4-universities-are-using-3d-printing-to-create-ears-cartilage-and-blood-cells/.
Shaddock, S. (2018, May 18). The vanguard: The coolest things on earth this week. *GE Reports*. Retrieved from https://www.ge.com/reports/5-coolest-things-earth-week-57/.
SkillsUSA additive manufacturing contest. (n.d.). Retrieved on July 19, 2018, from http://www.sme.org/skillsusa-additive-manufacturing-contest/.
Thurn, L. K., Balc, N., Gebhardt, A., & Kessler, J. (2017). Education packed in technology to promote innovations: Teaching additive manufacturing based on a rolling Lab. *MATEC Web of Conferences, 137*, 02013. doi: https://doi.org/10.1051/matecconf/201713702013.
Van Epps, A., Huston, D., Sherrill, J., Alvar, A., & Bowen, A. (2015). How 3D printers support teaching in engineering, technology and beyond. *Bulletin of the American Society for Information Science and Technology, 42*(1), 16–20. https://doi.org/10.1002/bul2.2015.1720420107.
Wohlers, T., & Gornet, T. (2014). History of additive manufacturing. *Wohlers Report 2014*. Retrieved on June 28, 2018, from http://www.wohlersassociates.com/history2014.pdf.
Workforce and economic development. (n.d.). Retrieved on June 28, 2018, from https://www.aacc.nche.edu/programs/workforce-economic-development/.
2016 Additive manufacturing body of knowledge update. (2016). Retrieved on June 28, 2018, from http://rapid3devent.com/wp-content/uploads/2013/03/AMBOK-Update-Executive-Summary.pdf.
3D digital design & manufacturing technology, certificate of proficiency. (n.d.). Retrieved on June 28, 2018, from http://catalog.tri-c.edu/programs/3d-digital-design-manufacturing-technology-certificate-proficiency/#programsequencetext.

Chapter Two

The Internet of Things

Sylvia Cox, Nita Johnson, and Melissa Price

The Internet of Things (IoT) is a growing phenomenon. The IoT allows devices to collect data, send information to the cloud for storage, and interact with each other. The IoT is entrenched in many facets of modern life.

Smart watches can measure heart rates, deliver emails, and send text messages because of the IoT. Personal banking is available via the IoT as deposits, withdrawals, and transfers, which can be completed with cell phones, laptops, and personal computers. Homes are now equipped with cameras, remote locks, and remote heating and air-conditioning controls, all linked to smart watches, smartphones, and other devices via the IoT. The autonomous vehicle is expected to be the next technological revolution, and the development and success of that technology depends on the IoT.

DATA STORAGE

The technological advances expected to occur in the future are growing rapidly because of the IoT. There is a massive amount of information that is readily available to a wide variety of users. There will be an estimated twenty billion recorded pieces of information stored in the cloud by 2020 as a result of the Internet of Things. The connectivity possibilities are endless (Hung, 2017).

Broadband internet connection is becoming more widely available, and the cost of connecting to the cloud is decreasing. IoT is the concept of connecting any device with the internet and then on to the cloud. Cell phones, coffeemakers, washing machines, headphones, lamps, and wearable devices will all contain sensors that connect to the internet and ultimately to the cloud for storage.

"We are also trying to understand what the many opportunities and challenges are going to be as more and more devices start to join the IoT. For now the best thing that we can do is educate ourselves about what the IoT is and the potential impacts that can be seen on how we work and live" (Morgan, 2014, para. 3).

Communication Models

There are communication models for the IoT that have been described by the Internet Architecture Board such as: Device to Device, which represents two or more devices that directly communicate with one another or through a server, over types of networks or the internet; Device to Cloud, which uses sensors to communicate to an internet cloud service; Device to Gateway, which communicates data through an intermediary between the sensor and a cloud computing service, and Back-End Data Sharing, which enables users to export data from a cloud service.

This technology provides multiple methods of communication, and that communication system is changing the marketplace as well as higher education. The possibilities for how this technology could shape society and the way humans and devices communicate and interact are just beginning to be understood. The possibilities for the future are boundless.

HIGHER EDUCATION AND THE IOT

How are community colleges and universities educating students about the IoT? What important hardware and software is necessary in order to support student learning via the IoT? How will teaching and learning be impacted by the IoT? What security risks does the IoT bring? What role should colleges and universities play in the advancement of IoT? The answers to all of these questions vary.

University research related to the IoT is broad and is usually defined by the discipline studying the technology. According to Dr. Benton Calhoun (2015), associate professor in the Electrical and Computer Engineering Department at the University of Virginia, "the internet of things means a lot of things to a lot of different people. It essentially refers to the idea that devices and objects on and around people are connected to the internet and its network" (2015, para. 4).

Innovative studies related to the IoT are developing at universities. Several technologies have the potential to significantly impact the educational environment in higher education. Potential areas of study include IoT security programs, which focus on the security required to protect IoT devices; IoT analytics, which analyzes the large amounts of data collected into the cloud; IoT management, which refers to the tools and processes capable of managing large amounts of data for retrieval, and IoT platforms, which integrate infrastructure components into a single product with a well-defined purpose.

IOT IMPACT

Many college majors will be impacted by the IoT. Programs of study in engineering, computer science, cybersecurity, and business will be impacted to a greater degree than others, but all graduates should have a thorough knowledge of the IoT. New careers will be developed to meet the workforce needs related to the rapid growth of IoT, such as data mining and data analysis for business and industry.

> Data mining operations in IoT environment plays a critical role in making smart systems capable enough to provide convenient and efficient services. Massive data generated or captured by IoT is converted into useful and valuable information by data mining operations. (Verma, Sood, & Kalra, 2017, p. 979)

"The exponential IoT technological advances have attracted the attention of researchers from various education disciplines. IoT has the potential to cause major disruption in variety of fields" (Verma et al., 2017, p. 977). Universities researching capabilities of the IoT are providing insights into the industry and all universities need to integrate IoT knowledge into required courses. "IoT is developing in two directions: increasingly smarter physical devices and environments and ubiquitous interconnection" (Banica, Burtesco, & Enescu, 2017, p. 54). This ubiquitous interconnection has the possibility to impact every sector of society.

CLEMSON UNIVERSITY

Clemson University (CU) in South Carolina is developing unique research in transportation related to IoT. The IoT has the potential to revolutionize the autonomous car research as it provides critical data to autonomous cars and other transportation devices.

Dr. Mashrur "Ronnie" Chowdhury is director of the United States Department of Transportation (USDOT) Center for Connected Multimodal Mobility (C2M2) and co-director of the Complex Systems, Analytics and Visualization Institute at Clemson University (CU). C2M2 is providing innovative research for the DOT using the IoT. The IoT can provide technology devices information that can be transmitted to DOT systems and create an Internet of Transportation.

C2M2 is a consortium of the five colleges in South Carolina and the South Carolina Department of Transportation (SCDOT). The colleges and SCDOT have banded together to establish a Tier 1 University Transportation Center. The team has been given a USDOT grant to research wireless communication devices and the field of transportation (M. Chowdhury, personal communication, June 8, 2018).

Adaptive Signal Control

The team of higher education institutions in C2M2 are Clemson University, Benedict College, South Carolina State University, the Citadel, and the University of South Carolina. The team is researching and collecting a variety of data using data sharing via the IoT. One current research initiative is exploring Adaptive Signal Control Algorithms for Connected Systems (M. Chowdhury, personal communication, June 8, 2018).

The proposed research will collect data on deployed connected vehicles (CVs) that are linked to traffic signal controls. The CVs and the traffic signals in the study will communicate via the IoT. The study will focus on determining necessary communication protocols for connectivity, type of data needed, data security, and the detection of vehicles and traffic jams by using information transmitted from traffic signals via the IoT (M. Chowdhury, personal communication, June 8, 2018).

Transportation and Air Quality

Another research initiative the team is exploring is the impact of transportation on air quality at elementary and middle schools in South Carolina. A combination of connected vehicles and environmental sensors will collect and monitor traffic flow and air pollutants at strategically selected schools in and around the state of South Carolina.

Uncertainty Quantification of Cyber-Attacks

The team is exploring the uncertainty quantification of cyber-attacks on intelligent traffic signals. The primary goal for the project is to develop and validate detection models for system control failures involving connected vehicle applications. The secondary goal is to establish long-term collaborative research between the C2M2 partners and Benedict College to provide research and career opportunities for underrepresented minority students in the field (M. Chowdhury, personal communication, June 8, 2018).

Ridesharing Services

Many foresee a future of shared mobility, where transportation network companies (TNCs) match passengers with similar origins and destinations on the fly so they can rideshare (M. Chowdhury, personal communication, June 8, 2018).

If feasible, shared mobility has the potential to reduce vehicle miles traveled (VMT), help the environment, reduce congestion, and reduce crash damage, injuries, and fatalities. Shared mobility may also provide lower-cost transportation that will particularly benefit those with low incomes (M. Chowdhury, personal communication, June 8, 2018).

Pedestrian Crossing Safety

Using data from pedestrian accidents, researchers will deploy image detection technology on corridors with more frequent pedestrian crash patterns to determine the extent of the crossing maneuvers on accidents. This study will seek to provide information based on data to provide the best safety prediction model for pedestrians. The model would support a cost/benefit analysis for short-term solutions to pedestrian fatalities and injuries (M. Chowdhury, personal communication, June 8, 2018).

Active Traffic Monitoring

A network of distributed cameras could be developed in areas that will map the location of vehicles throughout a network in real time. Allowing a vehicle to be tracked over several miles will provide a robust set of traffic parameters for a variety of applications, which include real-time traffic prediction, erratic maneuvering, dangerous driver identification, incident management, and a transportation network security (M. Chowdhury, personal communication, June 8, 2018).

Policy Needs

The CU research team will conduct a comprehensive search of the literature and document the safety incidences in the past ten years by utilizing the National Electronic Injury Surveillance System (NEISS) (M. Chowdhury, personal communication, June 8, 2018).

Effectiveness of Intermodal Facility Locations

Current logistics systems in the United States are inefficient, and the results of this inefficiency include wasted fuel, increased costs, and escalating congestion along roads and within urban centers. This project will explore fundamental elements of innovative infrastructure, parts of a connected logistics system, and functional features of this system that will be required to support a future process based on on-demand logistics (M. Chowdhury, personal communication, June 8, 2018).

Real-Time Classification of Vehicles

The goal of this project is to conduct a feasibility study on the development of software and hardware that will measure multiple transportation modes and assess vehicles by Federal Highway Administration (FHWA) classification. The research team will install several combined computer/camera systems to monitor the multimodal traffic in the proximity of the University of South Carolina campus.

This area has multiple transportation users, including pedestrians, mopeds, bicycles, motorcycles, passenger cars, trucks, trains, and buses. Along with the video data, additional traffic collection sources such as pneumatic tubes and Bluetooth will be used (M. Chowdhury, personal communication, June 8, 2018).

Railway Right-of-Way Monitoring

The first phase, a one-year project proposal, is to conduct feasibility studies and provide recommendations for the development of a Railway Right-of-Way Monitoring and Early Warning System. The feasibility study will seek to answer several questions:

How can drones and satellites be used to monitor the railway infrastructure? What infrastructure components can be monitored effectively, and what are the potential limitations of a RailMEWS in each case? What railway Infrastructure Monitoring Systems (IMS) are available today for integration with satellite and drone data? What are the desired functions and design parameters of an Early Warning System? What is the incremental investment needed to develop the RailMEWS system? (M. Chowdhury, personal communication, June 8, 2018).

Connecting Devices

The research that the team at Clemson University is doing depends heavily on the IoT. Connecting devices and sharing information via the IoT allows the transportation system in South Carolina to improve, but it also has possibilities for informing a larger audience. The technological advances that will result from this research will assist the industry with autonomous cars. Much of the concerns about autonomous cars would be addressed if multiple devices were communicating with railways, bridges, and roads.

Devices could be hosted in traffic signals, roads, and signs. The information collected in these devices would be helpful, but also the devices could communicate with each other in order to inform other autonomous vehicles what areas to avoid and other information that would allow the vehicles to avoid accidents (M. Chowdhury, personal communication, June 8, 2018).

BENEDICT COLLEGE

Dr. Gurcan Comert is a professor in physics and engineering at Benedict College (BC), in Columbia, South Carolina. BC is one of five higher education institutions partnering with the United States Department of Transportation (USDOT) Center for Connected Multimodal Mobility (C2M2). Dr. Comert is working to create a platform around connected, multimodal transportation technologies.

These connected devices use the IoT to create technologies that will radically change transportation systems and the industries that utilize the systems. Research at BC is focusing on the Networking of Systems and Pollution Emittances of Transportation (G. Comert, personal communication, July 12, 2018).

Network of Sensors

The current technology research focuses on the network of sensors for emissions. Presently sensors using the IoT can detect basic traffic data and pollutants. The sensors BC is testing are embedded on streets near the college. Traffic camera technology connected via the IoT is providing data to the research team via the cloud. As the research continues, Dr. Comert foresees possibilities for researching traffic pattern data that is collected via the IoT.

Dr. Comert's research team is collecting data using sensors at high traffic intersections near campus to collect emissions pollutants of the vehicles. The analysis of the data collected via the IoT can provide answers to pollution problems. As industries begin to access large amounts of data, analysis will be needed to convert the data into meaningful information (G. Comert, personal communication, July 12, 2018).

COMMUNITY COLLEGES AND THE IOT

Community college programs are impacted by the IoT. According to Grajek, "any successful institutional strategy must have a digital footprint" (2018, p. 14). The IoT requires immediate attention of leadership. Per Pierce, "Fifty-one percent of community colleges say they are actively considering the potential of the Internet of Things in their strategic planning" (2017, p. 16).

Community college students will come to campus with numerous devices, and they will expect to be able to interact with instructors and staff via the devices. Technology infrastructures need to be sufficient and growing. Bandwidth connections will need to meet the demands of the hundreds and thousands of devices that will be on community college campuses.

Administrators, faculty, and staff will have to consider privacy and security. They will need to manage many challenges associated with IoT, but the advantages of understanding, utilizing, and innovating with IoT are great for community college students. Teaching technology makes community college students more competitive in the workforce no matter their field of study (Pierce, 2017).

MIDLANDS TECHNICAL COLLEGE

Adrian Brown, CISCO telecom instructor at Midlands Technical College (MTC) in Columbia, South Carolina, shared insight on how the IoT is impacting programs at the college. "IoT is actually the Internet of Every Thing" (A. Brown, personal communication, June 7, 2018). Network systems connectivity across the internet is the core of the IoT. In today's modern society, cell phones and other smart devices communicate via wireless networks. As information is being transmitted via wireless networks, data is being collected (A. Brown, personal communication, June 7, 2018).

The rapid growth and utilization of the IoT has already brought many changes to society, and Brown believes there are many more to come. Cybersecurity is an emerging and evolving technology for IoT due to the potential ease to tap into personal and business devices or systems and hack information. Technology security is being taught at MTC to combat present threats.

However, as new devices are developed and launched, new issues will arise and the industry needs to be prepared to meet those challenges. Students in the IT fields will be working with technology devices and information to make sure that systems and information remain secure. Securing networks and centralized controls is an important factor when connecting devices to IoT (A. Brown, personal communication, June 7, 2018). Community college instructors like Brown are educating students about the IoT and the potential benefits and threats of the technology.

STANLY COMMUNITY COLLEGE

Kelly Caudle is the program head of Cisco Academy Support Center (ASC) at Stanly Community College (SCC), Albemarle, North Carolina, and a Southeastern Cisco hub trainer. Cisco Networking Academy is a global network of information technology (IT) skills and career building programs.

The community provides consistent standards and quality instruction in the field of IT. Academy Support Centers are leaders in the IT community and provide education, support, and guidance for those learning IT essentials in an online platform (Support and training, n.d.).

The Cisco Networking Academy program at SCC teaches networking and information technology skills to students in high school, community colleges, and universities. SCC serves 140 of these institutions throughout North Carolina, South Carolina, Virginia, Tennessee, Georgia, Florida, and Alabama. Additionally, SCC provides local courses that allow Stanly County residents and surrounding residents the opportunity to obtain advanced training (Academy support center—Cisco, n.d.).

Caudle provided information regarding courses provided by Cisco and the impact of IoT on information technology. According to Caudle, "IoT courses are being taught in South Carolina and North Carolina to colleges, universities and business partners" (personal communication, July 6, 2018). This technology is impacting every aspect of business and the careers students will enter. "IoT is [a] multidisciplinary discipline" (K. Caudle, personal communication, July 6, 2018).

IoT cannot be neatly contained in one course, area, or department. IoT knowledge impacts all programs and should be intentionally incorporated into course objectives and goals. The IoT study includes various majors, curricula, and fields of study across education (K. Caudle, personal communication, July 6, 2018).

Currently IoT is intensely integrated into computer engineering technology and electrical engineering technology programs. The IoT technology is commonly used in devices such as cell phones and cameras. Cisco has already developed live sensors for parking spaces that are connected to an app. This app can tell a person where parking spaces are available.

Smart homes and the IoT technology are already a part of the way many people live. Doorbells, refrigerators, laundry, and delivery systems using drones all connect to the IoT. The technology is effecting the innovation in many sectors of business and industry and many countries of the world. Cisco Networking Academy is already available in many languages and in many countries such as England, China, France, Japan, Netherlands, Russia, Portugal, and Spain. Intermediate levels of IoT courses include big data, analytics, and a hackathon playbook (K. Caudle, personal communication, July 6, 2018).

FUTURE IMPACTS

Changing technology will continue to impact higher education.

The New Media Consortium follows technology trends that are likely to affect colleges. The organization's 2017 Horizon Report pegged the Internet of Things as a significant development that will have a big impact on higher education in the next two to three years. (Pierce, 2017, p. 16)

IoT impact at community colleges and universities will be visible in the integration of strategic plans, in the leadership's urgency to adapt to the pace of change, and most importantly in the realization that the IoT must become a priority. Grajek reports that "the focus of information technology in higher education for 2018 is on remaking higher education, through four primary themes: Institutional Adaptiveness, Improved Student Outcomes, Improved Decision-Making and IT Adaptiveness" (2018, pp. 13–14).

Institutions that are able to successfully cultivate technology will be at an advantage. Community colleges that embrace the IoT movement will be able to provide immediate needs to business and industry as well as train professional technicians for the future. According to Pierce (2017), "The universe of objects containing microprocessors or embedded sensors capable of communicating and transmitting information across networks is called the Internet of Things, and it has enormous implications for community colleges" (p. 16).

Short Term (1–5 Years)

Innovators and entrepreneurs will continue to find ways to introduce IoT into businesses and industry. Agriculture, transportation, athletics, utilities, and many more will utilize IoT to inform practices and to conduct business. However, the infrastructure for IoT will continue to be stressed as the utilization of IoT increases (Friar, 2017). "Existing networks cannot support the addition of exponentially more devices, nor the near-instantaneous connection speed necessary for machine-to-machine communication. The next-generation network, 5G, must be designed to meet these requirements" (Friar, 2017, para. 2).

Technicians and engineers will be needed to meet the demand of maintaining the infrastructure and providing IT support for individuals and businesses. The basic course information that is being taught will need to increase and keep up with current changes in IoT for students to compete for jobs in the marketplace. In the near future, it could be a stand-alone major in community or technical colleges (K. Caudle, personal communication, July 6, 2018).

Within the next three to five years, the IoT will provide data that can be used to create predictive tools in traffic signals that would respond to the needs of traffic in an area. There are already some sensors being placed in high-traffic areas where there are a number of vehicle crashes. These sensors gather data related to heavy volumes of traffic, speed, and time of day.

In the short term, the IoT will allow states to use single switch technology for autonomous vehicles to share information about citywide traffic patterns, highway traffic patterns, traffic signal systems, and traffic safety.

Mid-Term (5–10 Years)

Research development needs will continue to grow as society explores ways to incorporate IoT into more devices and more uses. Within the next five to ten years, research on connectivity using drones and sensors to alert drivers of available parking spaces in a real-time cloud network will exist in large cities. This will mitigate searching for parking (G. Comert, personal communication, July 12, 2018).

Community colleges and universities need to focus on teaching cybersecurity to prepare for the enormous need to protect information in the cloud. Maintaining and managing cybersecurity networks will be a tremendous task in the IoT (M. Chowdhury, personal communication, June 8, 2018). Teaching technology with the growth of IoT will require curriculum and planning across many disciplines. Policy developments will be important. Within the next five to ten years, sensors will be developed for autonomous cars that will emulate the human mind (M. Chowdhury, personal communication, June 8, 2018).

There will need to be a methodology of safety and security procedures related to IoT. Teaching systems and delivery will live mainly in cloud management and network management (A. Brown, personal communication, June 7, 2018). Instructional methods and delivery will need to include IoT tools and techniques as well as knowledge-based curricula development related to the technology.

Long Term (10–20 Years)

In the next ten to twenty years, the IoT cloud will need constant monitoring for potential hacking. The cloud will need firewalls and other high-tech cybersecurity. New technology will be introduced to meet this need. All aspects of maintenance and security related to IoT will be needed. CU is working toward being an innovation hub such as Silicon Valley to meet the opportunities that IoT will continue to provide in the future.

Heterogeneous wireless communication (Het Net) is new technology being developed. Het Net will be needed for autonomous vehicles. In the future, dead zones can no longer exist, and there must always be communication and signals, because most, if not all, devices will be connected to IoT.

The emerging 5G network will be the optimal choice for connectivity. Data will be received from roadside devices, IT centers, social media, and wireless services through this network. This will also assist with cost and safety. Level 5 autonomous vehicles will exist and will depend on the IoT. There will be no steering wheel, and the vehicles will be fully automated (M. Chowdhury, personal communication, June 8, 2018).

The IoT will be integrated into all programs and disciplines. Courses such as Introduction to IoT, IoT Fundamentals, Connecting of Things, and Basics of Networking will be taught across all disciplines. Colleges and universities will also need to ensure that funding is available for lab kits and learning system toolkits to teach the fundamental skills needed to manage processes and devices that connect with the IoT (K. Caudle, personal communication, July 6, 2018).

ADVICE FOR ADMINISTRATORS

Administrators at community colleges and universities will need to prioritize the resources to address the needs of infrastructure and learning tools connected to the IoT. Grajek (2018) suggests that higher education leadership will need to reframe how the exponential occurrences in IoT will affect them.

> CIOs need to understand how to talk about technology in the language and context of education, research, administration, reputation, and risk. Presidents and provosts need to learn how to ask IT leaders the right questions about potential IT investments; CBOs need to help their institutions manage technology investments in addition to technology budgets; and boards need to ensure that technology is treated as a risk and a risk mitigate, as a capital investment, and as an agent of institutional transformation. (Grajek, 2018, p. 14)

Higher education instruction will look very different in a highly digital world. Grajek states that "remaking higher education in a digital world calls for everyone—students, researchers, instructors, administrators, librarians, technologists, business officers, all constituents—to accept that change is upon us and will not end. We are in an era of great change" (2018, p. 59). "The only thing constant is change. The pace of change is increasing and we have to ready the institution and our staff for that" (Grajek, 2018, p. 53).

As community colleges and universities strategically plan for the twenty-first-century student, they must prepare to educate students about the technology and prepare to use the technology to the benefit of the institution. Universities are deeply involved in educating and researching the various branches of wireless connectivity. Community college administrators and faculty need to find a way to be involved in this research (A. Brown, personal communication, June 7, 2018).

> Higher educators must teach broader ranges of courses on wireless eco-systems such as the Divergent of All Things and how the connectivity is deployed and research universities should partner with community and technical col-

leges. They also need to become aware of all the disciplines needed for the IoT. (M. Chowdhury, personal communication, June 8, 2018)

"There remains a great need for funding and opportunities in this area. BC has a vision for a problem-solving lab to assist agencies and businesses in the Midlands Technical College" (G. Comert, personal communication, July 12, 2018).

Partnerships in Higher Education

Community colleges and universities need to partner to continue the important research work that needs to be done and that will continue related to IoT. Engaging secondary partners is equally important. "Begin initial conversations with local high schools to build, sooner than later, pipelines and pathways beginning in the middle school to the colleges" (G. Comert, personal communication, July 12, 2018). "Host events to encourage and alert students of opportunities in STEM. Programmers will be needed for projects and students may be unaware of this career" (M. Chowdhury, personal communication, June 8, 2018).

Continuous Research

IoT needs and research will continue to evolve and change, but the demand for research will stay constant. "Stay on top of research and innovation" (M. Chowdhury, personal communication, June 8, 2018). A new major should be considered due to the multidiscipline majors of IoT programs. Cyber physical sciences would consist of electrical engineering technology (EET), civil engineering technology (CET), and mechanical engineering technology. All of these fields need to work together in the future to meet the demands that will arise because of the IoT (M. Chowdhury, personal communication, June 8, 2018).

"The US National Academy of Engineering identified ten criteria necessary for training tomorrow's engineers" (Chowdhury & Dey, 2016, p. 4). These criteria are: strong analytical skills; practical ingenuity in identifying and solving complex problems; creativity in defining the complexity of interconnected systems; effective communication skills to stakeholders; effective business and management skills; high ethical standards and professionalism; dynamism, agility, resilience, and flexibility to adapt to the rapidly changing engineering landscape; and lifelong learning to keep abreast with new knowledge and technologies (Chowdhury & Dey, 2016).

Community colleges and universities are going to have to aggressively focus on the technical advances that are coming. The IoT will bring rapid change to all industries. Community college and university administrators must make technology innovation and maintenance a key driver.

ADVICE TO STUDENTS

The best advice to students related to the IoT is simple. Gain as much exposure to opportunities in the field of IoT as possible. The IoT has proven to be more than meets the eye. "Expose students to this emerging technology and the endless possibility of jobs" (G. Comert, personal communication, July 12, 2018). "Become aware of all the disciplines needed for the IoT. The educational and employment needs of the future will be very broad" (M. Chowdhury, personal communication, June 8, 2018). Students will have many possibilities when it comes to jobs if students are knowledgeable and experienced with the many facets of IoT.

CONCLUSION

The IoT is rapidly becoming omnipresent. It will literally connect most everything to everything else. It has significant potential to make the world a better place to live and work. On the other hand, it has the possibility of further reducing any notion of privacy. However, the job forecast will be very positive as this technology will create the needs for a large workforce of cybersecurity individuals, data analysts, and new positions that, as of yet, have not been imagined.

CHAPTER SUMMARY

- The IoT will soon hold twenty billion pieces of information in storage.
- There are various communication models such as: Device to Device, Device to Cloud, Device to Gateway, and Back-End Data Sharing.
- Community colleges and universities will need to develop a variety of programs, such as cybersecurity, data mining, data analysis, and more in connection with the IoT.
- Clemson University is developing IoT research in connection with transportation.
- C2M2 is a consortium of five colleges, and the South Carolina Department of Transportation has developed a Tier 1 University Transportation Center.
- C2M2 is researching adaptive signal control, transportation and air quality, ridesharing services, pedestrian crossing safety, and active traffic monitoring.
- The goal of the C2M2 project is to conduct a feasibility study on the development of software and hardware that will measure multiple transportation modes.
- In phase 1, the C2M2 project will research railway right-of-way monitoring.

- The IoT will play a significant role in the research.
- At Benedict College, traffic pattern research data collected through IoT will be studied to ascertain the extent of emissions pollutants of vehicles at high-traffic intersections.
- Community colleges are developing training on IoT.
- Midlands Technical College in South Carolina is developing programs in cybersecurity.
- Stanly Community College in North Carolina offers programs through the Cisco Network Academy.
- IoT is commonly used in devices such as cell phones and cameras.
- IoT study is becoming part of the strategic planning of community colleges and universities in order to keep up with the development of IoT technology.
- In the next five years, IoT will be used in traffic control.
- Het Net is a new technology that will be used in autonomous vehicles.
- The emerging 5G network will be the optimal choice for connectivity.
- New courses and programs will be offered at community colleges and universities such as: Introduction to IoT, IoT Fundamentals, Connecting of Things, and Basic Networking, to name a few.
- Community college and university administrators will need to understand IoT and prepare their institutions to address the development and training opportunities the new technology will bring.
- Community colleges and universities need to partner to continue important research work that needs to be done in relation to IoT.
- The US National Academy of Engineering identified ten criteria necessary for training tomorrow's engineers.
- Students should gain as much exposure to opportunities in the field of IoT as possible.
- The IoT is rapidly becoming omnipresent, connecting most everything to everything else.

REFERENCES

Academy support center—Cisco. (n.d.). Retrieved on June 29, 2018, from https://www.stanly.edu/node/1206.

Banica, L., Burtesco, E., & Enescu, F. (2017). The impact of internet-of-things in higher education. *Scientific Bulletin—Economic Sciences 16*(1), 53–59.

Calhoun, B. (2015, April 6). "How can we really get to a trillion sensors" to power internet of things? *UVA Today*. Retrieved from https://news.virginia.edu/content/calhoun-how-can-we-really-get-trillion-sensors-power-internet-things.

Chowdhury, M. & Dey, K. (2016). Intelligent transportation systems—a frontier for breaking boundaries of traditional academic engineering discipline. *IEEE Intelligent Transportation Systems Magazine, 8*(1), 4–8. doi:10.1109/MITS.2015.2503199.

Friar, G. (2017, November 22). Gearing up for the internet of things: Workshop brings together academia and industry to explore how to prepare next-generation wireless for machine-to-machine communication. *MIT News.* Retrieved from http://news.mit.edu/2017/mit-workshop-gearing-up-for-the-internet-of-things-1122.

Grajek, S. (2018, January 29). Top 10 IT issues 2018: The remaking of higher education. *Educause Review,* 11–59. Retrieved from https://er.educause.edu/articles/2018/1/top-10-it-issues-2018-the-remaking-of-higher-education.

Hung, M. (Ed.). (2017). *Leading the IoT: Gartner insights on how to lead in a connected world.* Retrieved from https://www.gartner.com/imagesrv/books/iot/iotEbook_digital.pdf.

Morgan, J. (2014, May 13). A simple explanation of the "internet of things." *Forbes.* Retrieved from https://www.forbes.com/sites/jacobmorgan/2014/05/13/simple-explanation-internet-things-that-anyone-can-understand/#266c043a1d09.

Pierce, D. (2017). Understanding the Internet of Things. *Community College Journal, 88*(1), 14–19.

Support and Training (n.d.). Retrieved on June 27, 2018, from https://www.netacad.com/about-networking-academy/support-training/?p_auth=AH763DlM&p_p_auth=vkcZnnq4&p_p_id=resendscreenname_WAR_resendscreennameportlet&p_p_lifecycle=1&p_p_state=normal&p_p_mode=view&_resendscreenname_WAR_resendscreennameportlet_javax.portlet.action=resendScreenName.

Verma, P., Sood, S. K., & Kalra, S. (2017). Smart computing based student performance evaluation framework for engineering education. *Computer Applications in Engineering Education, 25*(6), 977–91. doi:10.1002/cae.21849.

Chapter Three

Autonomous Vehicles and Drones

Mark Roth and Renata Sims

The employment numbers, due to repeated publishing, have become ingrained in the lexicon of modern business. "The US economy needs to create roughly a million jobs per year just to keep up with growth in the size of the workforce" (Ford, 2015, p. xi). Assuming this fact to be true, the real question is, where are the jobs going to come from and in what form will the jobs take? Furthermore, what industry or combination of sectors will grow to the extent that millions of able-bodied people will find employment?

One answer to these questions might be autonomous vehicles: cars, trucks, and drones. Experts predict that the combination of these three industries will create hundreds of billions of dollars of revenue and millions of jobs. An additional critical question is, will there be trained employees in place when needed, so as not to hamper this explosive growth?

The chapter begins with the history of the respective industries, what milestones have been achieved, and what milestones still need to be accomplished. Challenges facing the industries are discussed, along with the effect those challenges may have on curbing the projected growth of the industry. An outlook is given for each sector on a short-term, medium-term, and long-term basis. Workforce development for each industry is highlighted and emphasized. Finally, what impact these industries will have on higher education and higher education's leaders is debated.

AUTONOMOUS CARS AND TRUCKS: PRESENT AND FUTURE

The odds are that if one picks up any newspaper or magazine, over a month's time, the individual will run into an article about autonomous cars, trucks, or buses. These futuristic vehicles have taken over the transportation sector thought by storm. It is important to cut through all the conflicting information and determine what the future of this form of transportation means to the average person. Most of the publications lead one to believe that within a few years' time, cars, buses, and trucks will not have steering wheels or drivers. While that may be disconcerting for some, especially with the news of the first autonomous driver death in 2016, it is essential to separate fact from fiction in the autonomous vehicle space.

Background

It is essential to understand the lexicon of the autonomous driving industry. There are, in fact, five levels of automation—and six, if one counts vehicles with no automation whatsoever. The levels are:

- Level 0 automation refers to cars with no automation.
- Level 1 automation refers to some small steering, acceleration, and braking tasks being performed by the car without human intervention, but everything else is entirely under human control.
- Level 2 automation refers to features like advanced cruise control or the original "autopilot systems" on Tesla vehicles; the car can automatically take set precautions, but the driver needs to stay alert at the wheel.
- Level 3 automation still requires a human driver, but the human is able to hand over some "safety-critical functions" to the vehicle under certain traffic or environmental conditions. This poses some potential dangers as the major tasks of driving are transferred to and from the car itself.
- Level 4 automation refers to a car that can drive itself almost all the time without any human input, but it might be programmed not to drive in unmapped areas or during severe weather.
- Level 5 automation refers to full automation under all conditions (*Trends* magazine, "The autonomous car," August 2017, p. 30).

With this understanding, the reader can readily see that there are no commercially available Level 5 autonomous cars on the market today. This is not to say that they do not exist. They do, but commercial deployment is probably years away.

> The high potential promise for consumers is derived from Level 3 cars that drive themselves for a large part of a person's highway commute or Level 4 cars that are almost fully autonomous within a well-documented metropolitan area. Today, when companies refer to their efforts to build "self-driving" vehicles, they are referring to Level 3 and Level 4 vehicles. (*Trends* magazine, August 2017, p. 30)

The rollout of these vehicles is somewhat nebulous. While most automobile companies believe that Level 5 cars are in the offing, the actual deployment is some years away.

Milestones

In the 2018 study conducted by the Society of Automotive Engineers, several questions were asked to try to understand the deployment of Level 5 autonomous cars.

- Question: In 2013, what was the highest level of autonomy of products that your company was developing?
- Answer: Level 0 was 35 percent; Level 3 was 7 percent; and Level 5 was 4 percent.
- Question: In 2018, what is the highest level of autonomy of products that your company is developing?
- Answer: Level 0 was 17 percent; Level 3 was 15 percent; and Level 5, was 26 percent. This is a 22 percent increased swing at the Level 5, compared to 2013.
- Question: In five years, what do you think will be the highest level of autonomy of products that your company will be producing?
- Answer: Level 0 was 33 percent; Level 3 was 18 percent; and Level 5 was 12 percent.

This data showed that the significant production of fully autonomous cars was years away (*Trends* magazine, 2017).

Challenges Facing the Industry

Rolling out fully autonomous cars has a number of challenges. These challenges come in the form of regulatory practices, technological issues, and changing driver perceptions.
On the regulatory side:

> In the United States, the major difficulty is overcoming the regulatory fragmentation caused by 50 states having different preferences on licensing, car standards, regulation, and privacy protection. Right now, car manufacturers and software developers face conflicting rules and regulations in various states. This complicates innovation because makers want to build cars and trucks for a national or international market. There also needs to be greater clarity regarding legal liability, data protection, and legislation to penalize the malicious disruption of autonomous vehicles. (West, 2016, p. 2)

On the technological side:

> Simultaneously, media reports of manufacturers overpromising capabilities of semi-automated driving features, driver misuse of their system, and of purported feature failure, were frequent. The year [2016] saw the first fatality related to a highly automated driving features in an accident related to self-driving vehicle testing and the first official investigation of potential defects on an automated driving feature. (Abraham et al., 2017, p. 1)

There are issues with the technology, but with hundreds of companies, large and small, working on autonomous systems, these hurdles will be overcome in the short term. User perceptions of fully autonomous cars are changing with the news of the death of a pedestrian by a fully autonomous car with a driver inside in 2018. Comfort or trust in full automation appears to be declining. While the shift away from trust in automation was observed across all age groups, it was particularly noteworthy in the younger half of the age ranges (Abraham et al., 2017).

The youth demographic was most open to automation in 2016. Since then younger respondents' confidence appears to have shifted, becoming more cautious. Although younger respondents are still somewhat more accepting of full automation than older respondents, the gap between older and younger adults' perception of automation is closing in the direction away from acceptance of automation (Abraham et al., 2017). There are some issues to overcome in the industry, but time is on the side of the manufacturer. In other words, Level 5 vehicles will not be deployed tomorrow.

OUTLOOK

The outlook for this industry is extremely positive. Auto manufacturers are pouring billions of dollars into to research, trying to move closer to Level 5 automation. Jobs are being created in numbers not witnessed in the auto industry since the inception of the assembly line. New companies are being formed. These companies are designed to research and manufacture the component pieces of the disparate systems now integral to every automobile.

Short Term (1–5 Years)

Companies are working toward autonomous cars as quickly as possible. Investments are being made in the technology that will pilot these vehicles. These investments are ongoing and will continue to drive the industry to heights heretofore unseen.

> In 2016, GM spent $581 million to acquire self-driving car startup Cruise Automation, and in July 2017 GM announced that it's building a new research and development facility for Cruise Automation, as well as adding 1,100 new jobs in that division. (*Trends* magazine, 2017, p. 31)

GM is not the only company spending money chasing the dream. "In February, Ford announced it was going to be investing $1 billion in Argo AI" (*Trends* magazine, 2017, p. 31). This vast amount of money is not going to be spent overnight. The funds will be disbursed through the short-term into the mid-term, which makes the outlook of this industry very strong.

Mid-Term (5–10 Years)

The industry will not have perfected Level 5 autonomous cars in five to ten years. However, this does not mean this industry will not be healthy. Level 3 and Level 4 cars will be purchased and deployed in the mid-term, with Level 5 cars being tested in the mid-term and deployed in the long term. The proximate result of this staged rollout will be a vigorous industry outlook for the foreseeable future.

> Well over 2 million Level 3, 4, and 5 autonomous cars will be on the road, worldwide, in 2025. BI intelligence, for instance, estimates that the number will be about 2.1 million. But, the fact that Tesla is already integrating upgradeable "self-driving" systems into all of its cars indicates that a worldwide population of 10 million or more, is likely. (*Trends* magazine, 2017, p. 35)

Long Term (10–20 Years)

A healthy future lies ahead for the auto, truck, and bus industries, as well as all the other ancillary industries connected with the move to autonomous cars, regardless of the level of automation. This robust prediction bodes well for higher education and workforce development.

IMPACT ON COMMUNITY COLLEGES

Short Term (3–5 Years)

It is evident by the mountains of investment pouring into the autonomous car field that the industry is going to remain strong through the short term. The companies making these investments have recognized the need for people to be trained in all aspects of the autonomous vehicle field. Federal grants are being given to community colleges to help educate faculty and students across the country in this new technology.

The National Science Foundation awarded a $750 million grant to Sinclair Community College to help train faculty and students in this field.

> The goal of the proposed project is to increase the autonomous vehicle technology experience and knowledge of automotive technology educators throughout the nation and address the growing need for qualified, knowledge-

able technicians with capacity to maintain and repair autonomous vehicles. (Navera, 2017, p. 1)

This grant is indicative of what is happening in community colleges. The companies need employees to research, build, and maintain these technological systems.

Mid-Term (5–10 Years)

In the mid-term, more and more people are going to be needed to repair these vehicle systems. Starting with Level 3 and up, this technology has to be installed, calibrated, and repaired at every level. The numbers of these vehicles deployed will be in the millions, if not tens of millions. "Who will repair and maintain these robotic and technological marvels?" (Adler, 2018, p. 1). The perceived shortage of workers who can fix these technologically advanced products is becoming a concern to the manufacturers.

> As a first mover in automated vehicle technology, Bosch is addressing a need that might be 5 or 10 years from reaching critical mass. But automakers, dealers, industry groups, and academics agree that a significant gap exists in education and marketing of careers for automated vehicle service technicians. (Adler, 2018, p. 2)

The industry perceives a shortfall in the workforce, and that must be addressed before the event occurs. This becomes the mission of the community college. Workforce development is the community college's stock in trade. However, Sinclair Community College cannot do this alone, as the industry is too big. Local community colleges across the land and around the world must react and create programs addressing this shortfall.

Long Term (10–20 Years)

In the long term, community colleges must be prepared to create the service tech workforce needed to deal with autonomous cars and trucks.

> Fixed operations directors at franchised dealerships express awareness, if not yet a sense of urgency, about the need to develop service techs who will work on automated vehicles. Each new model year brings more technology to lower-priced vehicles, along with increased fleet ownership. (Adler, 2018, p. 3)

Community colleges have to react now as the autonomous car industry continues to grow. This is not a situation in which a community college can play catchup to a growth industry. The situation demands a more strategic solution.

IMPACT ON UNIVERSITIES

Short Term (1–5 Years)

Universities are dedicated to the development of autonomous cars, trucks, and buses. Several institutions have developed robust programs conferring degrees at all levels. These institutions are at the forefront of autonomous car research. This phenomenon is not new; this research has been ongoing for quite some time.

> Driverless car powerhouse, Carnegie Mellon's robotics lab, has been one of the most innovative hubs of research on autonomous driving for more than 30 years. Just look at ALVINN, the self-driving car the university introduced in 1989. For many years, the lab's faculty members have been highly sought after by an automotive industry scrambling for talents—whatever it costs. (Rychel, 2017, p. 2)

Universities across the country are nurturing programs supporting the eventual rollout of all levels of autonomous cars.

Mid-Term (5–10 Years)

Again, depending on the automation level, deployment of these high-level cars is not going to be a reality in the short term. At the very earliest, Level 5 cars will be deployed in the mid-term and higher education must provide the personnel to staff this healthy industry. As Randy Cole, executive director of the Ohio Turnpike, has said:

> There are a lot of people who are really beginning to equate this with the advent of the horseless carriage and the emergence of both the telephone and the automotive industries. It's disruptive. It's exciting. And it has the potential for great economic benefit and quality of life. (Hulsey, 2017, p. 2)

The industry is going to make demands on higher education, and higher education has to be ready to answer the call with research, personnel, and innovative ideas to further the autonomous car's industry expectations.

Clemson University

The researchers attended a presentation on Friday, June 8, 2018, which was held at Clemson University, led by Dr. Mashrur "Ronnie" Chowdhury. Dr. Chowdhury is not only the director of the USDOT Center for Connected Multimodal Mobility, but he is also a professor in the Department of Civil Engineering.

> Clemson was one of 19 universities in the nation chosen by the U.S. Department of Transportation to lead a transportation center. Clemson was awarded a $1.4 million grant from the Department to open the center, which will focus on the development of technology to assist with traffic issues in South Carolina. Clemson civil engineering professor Ronnie Chowhurdy will lead the center and researchers from the University of South Carolina, Benedict College, The Citadel, and South Carolina State University will also be housed at the center. The resources from such a center have enabled the South Carolina team to make a major leap ahead in its efforts to further transportation research and promote education and workforce development. The center will form partnerships with industries in South Carolina and provide the incubation platform of a business ecosystem around the topic of connected multimodal transportation technologies to grow the economy of our state. (R. Chowbury, personal communication, June 8, 2018)

This center specializes in connected and autonomous cars. Dr. Chowdhury was extremely knowledgeable and passionate about this industry. Below are some of the points from his presentation:

> We work on how to use wireless communication in a new way. We develop algorithms to predict the future. For example, when you're going through the light, if you can predict when it will turn red, you can do amazing things. We are also developing predictive tools based on machine learning in which we will know when there will be an accident, when the light will turn red, and when there will be a traffic jam. We are developing driverless components, but the cars will be developed by car companies. There is a controller in the car that controls the steering and braking which acts as the brain. We have video cameras in the cars which act as the eyes of the driver, and there are audio sensors throughout the car that acts as ears. On the top of the car are sensors which are looking at the environment. These cars have all of the senses of a human driver. We are simply compensating for the entire whole human being. In Europe, they have automated cars, but the problem is they are very expensive because the cars need a large number of sensors. We did a study and observed that sensors can fail. When sensors fail, accidents occur. Our purpose at Clemson University is to make the autonomous cars low cost and also improve its reliabilities so the cars will not get into accidents so often. We are also looking at the cybersecurity aspect. (M. Chowdhury, personal communication, June 8, 2018)

Long Term (10–20 Years)

The industry has made projections, but some analysts believe in a longer-term outlook. The rollout of genuinely autonomous cars (Level 5) to the consumer market is probably many years away. David E. Cole, co-founder and chairman of AutoHarvest.org, stated:

> Companies are saying, "We're going to have something here in 2021 or 2019." It's leading the public to believe it's really close. The people who think, "I'm going to take a trip while sleeping in the back seat," that's probably 20 or 30 years away. (Hulsey, 2017, p. 3)

Regardless, the industry needs have to be met, and admittedly there is already a shortfall of talent. It is incumbent on higher education to muster the resources to keep tracking the automotive industry as it moves toward a Level 5 rollout.

WHAT LEADERS MUST DO

The autonomous car industry is embarking on a complete revolution in the transportation industry. If successful, this industry will change the face of transportation in the foreseeable future. Carla Bailo, assistant vice president of mobility research and business development at Ohio State University, put it like this:

> You've probably heard the statistic that traffic fatalities and incidents are going up. And the vast majority, in fact, 94 percent of those (accidents) are caused by human error. So really eliminating that human brain from the equation should come close to creating vision zero—zero traffic accidents and fatalities. (Hulsey, 2017, p. 3)

This is a call that leaders must answer, and unfortunately, higher education is behind the curve for workforce development for the autonomous car industry. Such training must be developed quickly.

ADVICE TO HIGHER EDUCATION ADMINISTRATORS

The field of autonomous cars is proliferating, and the future of the industry looks very strong. It is imperative that higher education take notice of the possible windfalls that may come from embracing this technology at every level. Some institutions have recognized the opportunity this industry represents, but the industry is demanding more research, more innovation, and most importantly, more people to fill much-needed positions.

DRONES OR UNMANNED AERIAL SYSTEMS

The State of the Industry

Drones are here to stay, and they are going to be one of the largest industries of the twenty-first century.

> Even if you have no immediate plans to buy a drone (yet), a lot of people do. In a few years, we've gone from a hobbyist niche to an estimated one million consumer-class, or small-business drones sold last year in the U.S. alone. Such a steep growth curve has all the earmarks of a new product category. (Mills, 2016, p. 1)

The critical question, in this case, is, although consumer growth seems robust, does the commercial or business drone industry have a future? Perhaps more importantly, will this future create the need for a healthy and growing workforce?

Is there a need for a commercial drone industry beyond the manufacturer of hobbyist unmanned aerial systems (UASs)?

> Venture capitalists have poured nearly a billion dollars into new drone companies (almost 90% of the money last year too), including deals led by storied venture giant Kleiner Perkins and the prescient tech team at Lux Capital. And that doesn't count private corporate spending on drones from Boeing and General Atomics to Intel and Qualcomm. (Mills, 2016, p. 1)

The answer becomes evident that not only is there a robust consumer market for drones, but the commercial/industrial market is exploding, as well. As a matter of fact, the growth in the industrial market is eclipsing the consumer market.

> A new Goldman Sachs analysis sees a cumulative $100 billion "total addressable market" over the next five years alone. India's RNR Market Research just released a 1,000-page analysis that concludes drones will be a $37 billion annual global business in a half-dozen years. The drone trade association, AUVSI, forecasts over $80 billion will be added to the U.S. economy for drone commerce in the coming decade. (Mills, 2016, p. 2)

This industry is here to flourish, in both the United States and the world. This industry represents an outstanding opportunity for the workforce of the future.

Milestones

The drone industry is growing and developing daily. It is essential to put this industry into perspective. Looking at a product life cycle, where is the industry currently?

> To use the obvious analogy (with the usual caveat about the limits of analogies) is today the equivalent to 1979, the year before Apple went public and became a driver and player in the PC revolution, or 2007 the year Apple launched the iPhone? (Mills, 2016, p. 5)

Growth in the industry, according to Mills, is at its infancy. Additionally, to place a more delicate point on the growth of this industry, adding some revenue numbers may sharpen the reader's perspective.

> Few would have imagined the transformation of unmanned aerial vehicles (UAV), commonly known as drones, from toys for adults to revolutionary machines for businesses, the military, cinema, maintenance groups, fire-fighters, health services, farming and so much more. As a result, UAV sales have shot up: in the U.S. alone they saw a 224% increase in the April 2016–April 2017 period alone. Recent PwC analysis has priced the overall market at a staggering $127 billion. (Moingeon, Chisholm, & Lafranc, 2017, p. 2)

The explosive growth is occurring now. However, to get to the lofty heights predicted by so many organizations, this level of growth will have to be sustained over the next five to ten years. The crucial caveat is that the industry as a whole has to ensure that nothing stands in the way of this projected growth, like excessive regulation or obstructionist policies created by governments around the world.

Challenges Facing the Industry

As with every industry, roadblocks occur; this fact holds true for the UAS industry, as well. "The future for drones is as much about policymakers and regulators as it is about the technologists" (Mills, 2016, p. 3). In the case of drones, those policymakers happen to be the Federal Aviation Administration (FAA). "If you buy a drone today, a microUAS, you not only need government permission to use it but how, when, and where you may use it" (Mills, 2016, p. 3).

Frustration is growing with the drone rulemaking at the FAA. Moreover, it is now believed that the process of rulemaking is hampering this robust industry growth rate and adoption. "Committee Chair, Senator David Vitter (R. LA) agreed, opening those hearings by noting that the FAA's failure to meet regulatory deadlines has limited the growth of the commercial drone industry" (Mills, 2016, p. 4).

The problem of burdensome regulation is not just a United States issue. In many countries, the regulations around drones can be seen as a stumbling block. However, in most cases, there are accredited pilot training courses, and there are defined processes to register commercial drones and obtain the operational go-ahead when needed. New rules by the U.S.'s Federal aviation administration in 2016 have streamlined the process of legally operating a UAV for commercial purposes. Within the first month of the FAA opening its registration site, 300,000 drones were registered. (Moingeon et al., 2017, pp. 3–4)

Challenges do exist in the industry. However, the FAA has now made concessions to its own bureaucracy's rulemaking to speed up the rollout of drone statutes and laws. These FAA changes will help keep the industry growing and on track to reach the predicted lofty revenue numbers.

OUTLOOK

Industry Projections

Change is now the operative word in the drone marketplace. New manufacturers and a new rationale for using these soon-to-be ubiquitous machines are reaching the market daily. As mentioned above, this growth has been supported by the actions of the FAA. "The popularity of drone utilization has been driven by a relaxation of regulatory restrictions and the combination of maturing payload technologies intermixed with falling drone prices" (Wolf, 2017, p. 2).

This change in course by the FAA is creating a seismic shift by companies now entering the drone space. Historically, and to the present day, drone spending was regulated solely to the military. However, that is now changing and changing quickly.

The drone market today is still dominated by military spending (as was the case for computing at the dawn of that age). According to Goldman and others, precision agriculture is the big commercial application that has immediate potential to become a multi-billion dollar industry alone. Other applications are limited only by imagination and the inevitable and rapid maturation of underlying technologies. They include such things as emergency services, ecological surveys, journalism, surveying, cinematography, and of course package delivery. (Mills, 2016, p. 2)

This growth is not just predicted for the United States:

In Europe, the SESAR (Single European Sky ATM Research) European Drones Outlook Study reported: "The growing drone marketplace shows significant potential with European demand suggestive of a valuation in excess of

10 billion euros annually, in nominal terms, by 2035 and over 15 billion euros annually by 2050." (Wolf, 2017, p. 4)

Short Term (1–5 Years)

The proximate result of this growth is readily apparent. The growth of this industry is happening now in the short term. This is supported by the fact that venture capital firms are moving into the sector with one billion dollars last year. Moreover, Goldman Sachs predicted the total market would reach 100 billion dollars by 2021 (Mills, 2016). Hence the short-term outlook for the industry looks good.

Mid-Term (5–10 Years)

The mid-term outlook also looks robust, with industry analysts predicting that in the United States alone, approximately 80 million dollars will be added to the economy (Mills, 2016).

Long Term (10–20 Years)

Finally, in the long term, European analysts predict industry growth rates surpassing 150 percent. If anticipated changes with visual-line-of-sight (VLOS) and beyond-visual-line-of-sight (BVLOS) come into being, the new growth rates will eclipse those already predicted (Wolf, 2017).

IMPACT ON COMMUNITY COLLEGES

Community colleges have long had three significant missions: (a) college transfer, (b) vocational education, and (c) community service (Bers, Head, & Palmer, 2014). Two of the previous three points have a direct influence on workforce development. Presumably the student graduates and then transfers to a four-year institution to continue with the student's studies. However, the two points that have to do with workforce development will be directly affected by the proliferation of the drone industry. Community colleges must react to this new industry and develop programs to train the workforce employed by this industry.

One of the unique characteristics of the UAS industry is that both curriculum and continuing education programs will have to be created to serve the needs of this burgeoning industry.

Workforce Development

Short Term (1–5 Years)

In 2011, the chairman of the Gallup Organization published a book entitled *The Coming Jobs War* (2011). Chairman Clifton mentioned that the biggest problem facing the United States, and the world for that matter, is the lack of good jobs. "A good job is a job with a paycheck from an employer and steady work that averages 30+ hours per week. Global labor economists refer to these as formal jobs" (Clifton, 2011, p. 2). The point is that the newly developing drone industry is providing additional jobs on a daily basis for those who are qualified and ready to work. It is up to community colleges to provide this new workforce.

The researchers conducted an interview on June 12, 2018, with Brian McGuire, the vice president of sales and marketing from CrossFlight Sky Solutions. CrossFlight Sky Solutions is a company with a bifurcated mission. First, the company flies commercial drones for others who need aerial footage or have to something to inspect, such as a tower or private residence roof. Second, the company provides instructors and curriculum for colleges that want to start drone programs.

The interview covered all aspects of CrossFlight's business and the future of the drone industry. Mr. McGuire was extraordinarily knowledgeable and forthcoming and was extremely excited about both the drone industry and CrossFlight's offerings within the field. He responded to a number of questions posed by the researchers.

- Question: Should the distinction be made between commercial and private drones?
- Answer: Yes, absolutely yes! Part of the biggest issue, and the biggest challenge to the FAA, and to commercial drone companies such as ours, is the public differentiating between business use of a drone and what we call hobbyist use of a drone. They are very much a different set of standards, a different set of policies, and a diverse set of regulations which you need to follow.

    If you are flying a drone for any commercial purpose at all, your pilot needs to be what's called a FAR Part 107 certified pilot. They have to take an FAA exam, which certifies them and makes sure that they understand that the FAA is looking at them as a pilot. Instead of piloting a manned aircraft, you are now piloting an unmanned aircraft. You almost have to know the same things, you have to understand airspace, you need to understand airport operations, and you need to know how to read airspace maps. You need to understand weather and physiological conditions.

> If you put a million of these drones up in the air, you need to make sure that you know where the helicopters are going to be, is there a hospital nearby, is there a military base nearby, where is the closest commuter airport, and these are all obviously very serious situations. The hobbyist is somebody who can take their drone out in their backyard, put it up in the air about 80 to 100 feet, take nice pictures and video of their house and their yard, and never do anything with it; it's just for fun. There's a distinct difference, and that's what the FAA is trying to make sure people understand (B. McGuire, personal communication, June 12, 2018).

- Question: Please put on your futurist glasses. Where do you think you're going to be in three years?
- Answer: Our company was originally founded by a retired FAA administrator, and he originally got into this business because he thought that there would be a lot of companies out there that needed pilots, for example, bridge companies that needed inspections, tower companies, cell phone, electrical, and radio tower companies that needed inspections, construction companies that needed aerial data, marketing companies that needed aerial video, but what we found is, yes, that's true, but the truth is, there are more people that want to be trained to be pilots, because of the need.

> So 90 percent of what we're doing is holding education and training classes, and seminars, to train pilots, so they can go back to their jobs, and use drones for their jobs. For instance, we do a lot of training in the construction industry. We do a lot of training for Realtors and photographers. We do a lot of training for land preservationists that want to watch over and monitor large pieces of land.
>
> We do a lot of training for electrical tower guys, electrical power guys. Instead of climbing up and down electrical powers poles, power lines, they can fly their drone, inspect it, even use thermal imaging to see where some of the hotspots are and figure out what needs to be done, what parts they need, and then go up and fix the tower. The training and education aspect of this industry has just absolutely blown up because there's going to be such a need for drone pilots in almost every industry. (B. McGuire, personal communication, June 12, 2018)

- Question: When looking at workforce development, there's a huge opportunity in this field, correct?
- Answer: Tremendous opportunity. Aside from what you hear with the Amazons and the FedExes, that want to deliver packages, drones are being used in law enforcement, they're being used by fire departments, they're

being used in emergency management situations, they're being used by civil engineers, surveyors, construction companies, photographers, Realtors, and so on and so on (B. McGuire, personal communication, June 12, 2018).
- Question: Where do you see the main workforce developing in the short term? What do they need the most?
- Answer: I think right now, it's in the construction field. I think it is in the engineering field. I think it's in the surveying field. Surveyors are still doing surveying the way they did thirty years ago. They send two guys out with a couple of staffs, they pace off ten paces or fifty paces, they mark it, and they do it again, and they just keep going until they cover the property. You can survey a thousand acres using a drone in an hour, whereas it would take two surveyors' weeks (B. McGuire, personal communication, June 12, 2018).

In the short term, it is apparent that because the industry is snowballing, pilots are in short supply, and that is where CrossFlight Sky Solutions has found its niche. Mr. McGuire has found that community colleges are the ideal training provider for these pilots. The company currently has fifteen community colleges under contract for pilot training.

Mid-Term (5–10 Years)

- Question: Are there jobs in the industry other than for pilots? What are the mid-term prospects, for example, in five to ten years?
- Answer: There are really three tiers of jobs, and the time frames aren't exact as to when we need these positions; the industry is moving much faster than anyone thought. The next tier, beyond the pilots, will be either the repair people or programmers. We see some small, they're called small aircraft, repair or small aircraft mechanics, and the way that drones are built right now, I'm not going to say it's similar to a model car, but it's one step up from a model car. It's made with a whole bunch of parts that are put together: the rotors, the battery, and the camera.

> Some of these drones have 20-megapixel cameras and can shoot video in ultra HD. And sometimes they crash, and when they crash, they need to be put back together again. So, for our company, we deal with a couple of service places in South Carolina, where we send our drone off to, and they can either fix it, or you have to buy a new one.
>
> But yes, that's absolutely going to be an opportunity as well, for those people that like to take things apart and put them back together again. With the growth of the industry, worldwide there are going

to be a lot of these repair and replace jobs available (B. McGuire, personal communication, June 12, 2018).

Long Term (10–20 Years)

When asked about the long-term prospects in the industry, McGuire was quick to point out that all positions are available now, but the number of openings will change with the growth of the sector.

Many community colleges are leading the way in drone workforce development. Sinclair Community College in Dayton, Ohio, is one such institution. The college has developed a certificate program in Unmanned Aerial Systems. The one-year certificate takes between thirty and thirty-three hours to complete and includes courses named "Introduction to Unmanned Aerial Systems" and "UAS Remote Sensing & Analysis," among others.

The school also has an Associate of Applied Science Degree in Unmanned Aerial Systems. Both programs allow their students to gain operational hours flying in the world's first dedicated UAS indoor flying pavilion on the Sinclair College campus.

The researchers talked with Ryan Palm, the program coordinator for unmanned aerial systems, regarding his thoughts about the future of workforce development in the UAS industry.

- Question: Where are the jobs going to be in this industry, and what are you training your students to do in the industry?
- Answer: Our students will all be pilots of course, but the jobs long-term (long-term jobs) will be in programming. You are not going to have one pilot to one drone ratio. You are going to have programmers programming any number of drones, and they will take off, fly the programmed route, complete their mission, and return to base. That is the future of this technology. We need pilots now, but we need more programmers for the future (R. Palm, personal communication, June 20, 2018).

These thoughts support the figures put out by the FAA: "The FAA anticipates its hassle-free regulations could generate more than $82 billion for the U.S. economy and create more than 100,000 new jobs over the next ten years" (Wolf, 2017, p. 3). These figures are welcome because they bode well for the economy for the long term. Moreover, if community colleges move toward offering programs to teach and train the workforce for this booming industry, the institutions' futures look bright, as well.

IMPACT ON UNIVERSITIES

Community colleges are not the only institutions of higher education entering the UAS space. Several universities have also started programs that are getting attention for students and employers alike. There are universities offering bachelor's-level training and master's-level training, and some universities even have doctorate-level training.

Admittedly, some of these degrees are heavily based on engineering and repairing drones ("15 Best," 2018, p. 1). It is understandable why these programs are growing, due to the heady predictions about the industry as a whole. The difficult decision for the potential student is whether or not the universities provide enough additional value to make attending the institution worthwhile.

Short Term (1–5 Years)

The website SuccessfulStudent.org has developed an article extolling the best drone training colleges. The material is informative, giving rationale for studying in the field, using evidence of need, and discussing the focus that the U.S. military is placing on the field. "The U.S. budget for drone warfare has increased from $667 million in 2002 to more than $3.9 billion, according to the Congressional Research Service. The number of drones in military service has increased from 167 to nearly 7,500" ("15 Best," 2018, p. 1).

The salient point is that many colleges have recognized the need for UAS pilots, programmers, and engineers in the short term, and those institutions that have not joined the effort are getting left out of one of the fastest-growing industries in today's economy.

Mid-Term (5–10 Years)

In the mid-term (5–10 years), the UAS industry will continue to grow. Drones will become ubiquitous, and demand will continue to skyrocket within the industry.

> If you think about it, the great number of different ways you can use drones, from doing mapping and surveying to mammal monitoring, package delivery, and agricultural spraying, means that many different businesses see ways to improve safety for their employed, reach more customers, reduce costs, and other benefits from the technology. (Bohi, 2018, p. 61)

It is apparent that the mid-term outlooks for this nascent industry are indeed robust.

Long Term (10–20 Years)

The long-term outlook for the industry is bright. The research and recent changes to the Federal Aviation Administration regulations contributed the measurable increase in drone activity over the past year. The proximate result of this is that drone pilots will surpass the number of flyers who currently hold a manned pilot's license (170,000) within a year (Bohi, 2018, p. 62). This early growth in the industry will create stronger, more robust growth in the long run, spawning new industry growth for the foreseeable future.

An interesting note: The researchers have found that new uses for drones are being discovered almost daily, driving entrepreneurship. "A great deal has been happening with drones in the past 12 months. The electrical power industry is expanding the use of UASs for high-risk tasks and the drone-asa-service marketplace" (Wolf, 2017, p. 4). This growth in innovation enhances the long-term outlook of the industry.

ADVICE TO HIGHER EDUCATION ADMINISTRATORS

Leaders make decisions, often at the height of uncertainty. However, in this case, the longevity of the drone industry is assured, and it will be one of the fastest-growing industries over the next twenty years. "By all indicators, the use of drones is not a passing phase. It's expected that nearly every industry either already is using drones or will be impacted by the use of drones in the near future" (Bohi, 2018, p. 60).

The critical factor is the breadth of the industry. It is going to affect nearly every segment of business and government. Because of this fact, everyone in a leadership role in higher education has to consider entering this field. While evidence may seem to indicate that entering the field now is late, there is still time to become involved. The crest of the industry has not yet been reached and will not be reached until at least the mid-term, and the drone industry will only then be achieving the industry's projections.

The long-term outlook for this industry shows that it will be growing exponentially for many years. Again, considering the breadth of the drone industry, industries and consumers will be affected. Therefore, it is incumbent upon higher education leaders to provide training and education to support this nascent, booming industry.

CONCLUSION

Autonomous vehicles and drones are two industries with very bright futures. Colleges, universities, and businesses are driving these industries forward to untold heights. There is one caveat: Both industries have a dramatic need for people to feed the growth projected over the next twenty years.

The seminal question here is, how can higher education be an integral part of this growth? Perhaps, more importantly, failing to plan for industry needs by not educating this future workforce will hamper both industries and slow the rollout of these technologies. This would be a detriment not only to the United States but to the world as a whole. The industry and higher education must work to collectively meet the demands of the new technologies.

CHAPTER SUMMARY

- The notion of autonomous cars, trucks, and buses has taken the transportation sector thought by storm.
- In the autonomous vehicle lexicon, there are five levels of automation and one level of no automation; the levels are designated by level 0 through level 5.
- There are no commercially available level 5 autonomous cars on the market in the United States in 2018.
- There are challenges facing the autonomous car industry such as those on the regulatory side and the technology side.
- Because of the death of a pedestrian by a fully autonomous car with a driver inside in 2018, the comfort and trust in full automation appears to be declining at the moment.
- The outlook for this industry is extremely positive.
- The automotive industry is working toward autonomous cars as quickly as possible.
- At present it is felt that it will take more than five to ten years for the autonomous car to be perfected.
- It is predicted that well over two million level 3, 4, and 5 autonomous cars will be on the road, worldwide, by 2025.
- Federal grants are being given to community colleges to help educate faculty and students across the country in the autonomous vehicle technology.
- More and more people are going to be needed to repair these vehicle systems in the next five to ten years.
- In the long term, community colleges must be prepared to create the service tech workforce needed to deal with autonomous cars and trucks.
- Many universities are dedicated to the development of autonomous cars, trucks, and buses.
- Clemson University was one of nineteen universities in the nation chosen by the United States Department of Transportation to lead a transportation center.

- Clemson was awarded a $1.4 million grant from the Department of Transportation to open a center, which will focus on the development of technology to assist with traffic issues in South Carolina.
- In Europe they have automated cars, but the problem is that they are very expensive because the cars need a large number of sensors, and often the sensors fail, which leads to accidents.
- It is incumbent on higher education to muster the resources to keep tracking the automotive industry as it moves toward a level 5 rollout.
- It is imperative that higher education takes notice of the possible windfalls that may come from embracing this technology at every level.
- Drones are here to stay, and they will be one of the largest industries of the twenty-first century.
- The drone industries will flourish in both the United States and the world.
- This industry represents an outstanding opportunity for the workforce of the future.
- Frustration is growing with the drone rulemaking at the FAA.
- The total market for the drone industry has been predicted by Goldman Sachs to reach $100 billion by 2021.
- European analysts predict drone industry growth rate surpassing 150 percent.
- Very different standards, policies, and regulations will end up governing commercial and private drones.
- For commercial use, the drone pilot needs to be certified.
- Drones are being used in a wide variety of business and industry applications, such as by Realtors and in land preservation, electric power inspection, and the like.
- In the short term, the main workforce will most likely be in the engineering field.
- There will be need for a workforce of technicians for drone maintenance and repair.
- Many community colleges are leading the way in drone workforce development.
- Some universities have already started programs offering bachelor's- and master's-level training, with a few providing doctoral-level education.
- The long-term outlook for the drone industry is bright, as new uses for drones are being discovered almost daily, driving entrepreneurship.
- Higher education administrators can rest assured of the longevity of the drone industry; it will be one of the fastest-growing industries over the next twenty years.
- The long-term outlook for the drone industry shows that it will be growing exponentially for many years.
- Autonomous vehicles and drones are two industries with very bright futures.
- Failing to plan for industry needs by not educating this future workforce will hamper both industries and the rollout of these technologies.

REFERENCES

15 best drone training colleges. (2018). Retrieved from https://successfulstudent.org/15-best-drone-training-colleges/.

Abraham, H., Reimer, B., Seppelt, B., Fitzgeraid, C., Mehler, B., & Coughlin, J. F. (2017). *Consumer interest in automation: Preliminary observations exploring a year's change* [White Paper]. Cambridge, MA: Massachusetts Institute of Technology, AgeLab.

Adler, A. L. (2018, February 19). The hurdles of fixing automated vehicles. *Fixed Ops Journal*, 1–11. Retrieved from http://www.autonews.com/article/20180219/RETAIL05/180219994/self-driving-car-repair.

Bers, T. H., Head, R. B., & Palmer, J. C. (2014). *Budget and finance in the American community college* (Number 168, Winter ed.). San Francisco, CA: Jossey-Bass.

Bohi, H. (2018, January). Welcome to the drone age: Oil, gas, engineering, construction use UAVs to reach the unreachable. *Alaska Business Monthly, 34*(1), 60–64.

Clifton, J. (2011). *The coming jobs war*. New York: Gallup Press.

Ford, M. (2015). *Rise of the robots: Technology and the threat of a jobless future*. New York: Basic Books.

Hulsey, L. (2017, September 26). 5 things experts say about self-driving cars. *Dayton Daily News*, 1–8. Retrieved from https://www.daytondailynews.com/news/national/things-experts-say-about-self-driving-cars/yMkRhSuE0vOSPPH7PGsUjM/.

Mills, M. P. (2016, March 23). Drone disruption: the stakes, the players, and the opportunities. *Forbes*, 1–7. Retrieved from https://www.forbes.com/sites/markpmills/2016/03/23/drone-disruption-the-stakes-the-players-and-the-opportunities/#7815e4ac7d0b.

Moingeon, B., Chisholm, L., & Lafranc, E. (2017, December 7). The day of the drone: How flying robots are revolutionizing business. *Forbes*, 1–4. Retrieved from https://www.forbes.com/sites/hecparis/2017/12/07/the-day-of-the-drone-how-flying-robots-are-revolutionizing-business/#bb1b3ab93a00.

Navera, T. (2017, May 26). Exclusive: Sinclair gets a big grant for new driverless cars program. *Dayton Business Journal*. Retrieved from https://www.bizjournals.com/dayton/news/2017/05/26/exclusive-sinclari-gets-big-grant-for-new.html?s=print.

Rychel, A. (2017). 7 Universities that are pushing the boundaries of autonomous driving. Retrieved from https://www.2025ad.com/latet/top-universities-for-autonomous/driving/.

The autonomous car industry emerges [*Trends* magazine]. (2017, August). *Trends* magazine, 29–36.

West, D. M. (2016). *Moving forward: Self-driving vehicles in China, Europe, Japan, Korea, and the United States* [Brookings Institute Study]. Washington, DC: Brookings Institution.

Wolf, G. (2017, April). Drones get a new flight plan: The relaxing of rules and regulations has had a positive impact on commercial drones. *Transmission & Distribution World, 69*(4), 2–7.

Chapter Four

Personal Robots

Mark Roth and Renata Sims

This chapter covers the field of robotics and, more specifically, personal robots. Both industrial and personal robots are included to give the reader a perspective on the ubiquitous nature of robots and the direction in which the field is going. There is a unique synergy in the robotics field. New technology flows freely between industrial robots and personal robots, creating advances in both segments almost simultaneously. The efficacy of the predictions made by experts in the field is discussed and compared to the actual rollout and acceptance of robots both in the industrial and personal setting.

The size of the market and growth predictions are included in the chapter to support some of the conclusions drawn about the future of the workforce and possible courses of study that would need to be undertaken to obtain an advantage in the industry. Conclusions are drawn as to the relative worth of pursuing training programs to develop the workforce for this no-longer-nascent industry.

ROBOTS AND ROBOTICS: PAST, PRESENT, AND FUTURE

Robotics is a topic captivating the world with its seemingly endless potential, a topic dominating from big business to the family home. Along with its engrossing nature comes negative discourse.

> In 2013, researchers at the University of Oxford's Martin School conducted a detailed study of over seven hundred US job types and came to the conclusion that nearly 50% of jobs will ultimately be susceptible to full machine automation. (Ford, 2015, p. 119)

This job loss premise has been in existence almost as long as robots have been in existence.

However, two points can be made from these forecasts and the new technology entering the industry. First, the predictions of the human worker's demise were and are incorrect, both then and now. Second, new technology coming into the robotic landscape may turn those incorrect forecasts to prescient projections as the field moves into the twenty-first century.

It is essential when talking about robotics to define the field. For the purposes of this chapter, the researchers are discussing actual robots. This chapter covers the scope of personal and industrial robots to compare trends in the two industries.

> Intelligent robots are an ideal, a vision. All one has to do to see the intelligent robot model is to look in a mirror. Ideally, all intelligent robots move safely, dexterously, smoothly, precisely, using multiple degrees of coordinated motion and do something like a human but that a human now doesn't have to do. They have sensors that permit them to adapt to environmental changes. They learn from the environment, or from humans without making mistakes. They mimic expert human responses. They perform automatically, tirelessly, and accurately. They can diagnose their own problems and repair themselves. They can reproduce, not biologically, but by making other robots. (Hall, 2001, p. 1)

Hall goes on to say that "of 100 engineering or scientific readers of this paper, perhaps only one is capable of designing and constructing an intelligent robot in their working lifetime of 30 years" (Hall, 2001, p. 4). This perhaps shows the reader why, despite the heady predictions, the robotics field has been slow to grow and has not achieved the predicted level of acceptance and share of the workforce.

PRESENT: ROBOTS COMMUNICATING WITH HUMANS

Robots are being created and used in a variety of ways, such as rehabilitation, assisting in eldercare, interacting with children, and other educational applications or functions. Throughout the years, robots have transitioned from assisting on manufacturing assembly lines to having intellectual conversations with humans. This area is still being perfected, and some critics are very uncomfortable with this premise.

> The question, though, is whether we actually want an artificial intelligence (AI) program (installed in a physical robot) that will enable a robot to have realistic human conversation with us. How much do we want their linguistic abilities—and functions—to be the same as found in mature human language users. (Baron, 2015, p. 262)

Technology has advanced throughout history, but society may not be ready for the next step, communicating with robots.

> How much authenticity do we want in our conversations with robots? Admittedly, it is always a gamble trying to predict potential technologies and future tastes. (Twenty-five years ago, few of us could have envisioned billions of people pecking out typed messages on phones rather than talking on the same devices.) But given current social sensibilities, it seems likely that at least in the near term, in building social robots, we will design them to do our bidding, not to be our conversational equals. We will be more prone to welcome informational and empathetic functions from social robots than their exercising social control or critique. (Baron, 2015, p. 263)

Some skeptics may say that they are not quite ready for this kind of human interaction with a robot, but soon this will become second nature.

Caregivers, Eldercare, and Robots

Caring for a loved one is always challenging, and it is extremely taxing on the caregiver. Society focuses on providing care for children and the elderly, but rarely for the caregiver.

> "Who will care for the caregivers?" Approximately 40 million Americans are doing just that. It takes a financial toll. Family caregivers lose more than $300,000 in wages and benefits over their lifetime because of the interruption in employment they experience providing care. In addition, family caregivers are often unhealthier and experience more emotional stress than their non-care-giving counterparts. ("Are Robots the Next Eldercare Trend?", 2018, p. 16)

"Caregivers normally neglect taking care of themselves because they feel that the loved one is more important" ("Are Robots the Next Eldercare Trend?", 2018, p. 16). There are instances when caregivers pass away before the loved one whom they were taking care of because they neglect themselves. This is why robot companions are instrumental for all involved. "Robot companions are already a big hit in some children's hospitals and eldercare facilities to help young and old people alike combat loneliness" ("Are Robots the Next Eldercare Trend?", 2018, p. 16).

> Some robots can help remind seniors to take their medication or tell them when it's time to eat. Some help mop the floors and do chores that seniors are unable to do, helping them age in place as they wish. And some robots provide social interaction and options to play games with seniors to keep them mentally stimulated throughout the day. Others even provide directions on how to cook different meals. ("Are Robots the Next Eldercare Trend?", 2018, p. 16)

With all of the menial tasks that robots can provide, not all Americans are comfortable with robots coming into their homes providing these services. "A report stated that 59% of Americans surveyed weren't excited about the prospect of a robot helping their loved ones, 40% said they were open to the option" ("Are Robots the Next Eldercare Trend?", 2018, p. 16).

Personal Robots in Japan

Robotic applications are already present in some countries, especially in regard to the health-care industry.

> Japan is already using robots to assist the elderly. Given their aging population (and low birth rate), the Japanese have been working for years to develop robots that can tend to the elderly. Such robots, like Frank's, presumably do not take "no" for an answer. As rates of older people with dementia rise around the world, we can easily imagine the utility of social robots that not only offer information but also provide companionship (and control) using ordinary language. (Baron, 2015, p. 262)

Will humans be comfortable taking orders from robots?

> When a person tells us it is time to eat or take medicine, we generally have the choice of whether or not to comply. We can ignore the command, shout "Leave me alone" or perhaps leave the room. If the communication is written, we can decide not to respond or even block further messages from the individual intruding on our personal space. As social beings, we learn how to navigate our way around those whose expectations of us we do not wish to fulfill. It is unclear that we would welcome robots that refuse to leave us in peace. (Baron, 2015, p. 262)

Humanoid Robots and Children

In other countries and in some parts of the United States, robots are used in classrooms to assist teachers with students.

> Although in its infancy, humanoid robots have a track record in the K–12 classroom, from teaching English to South Korean children, in England helping autistic, and in the U.S. teaching foreign languages to preschoolers. Robots are also used as remote controlled teachers when a human teacher at a remote location controls the robot's performance in class as is the case at a school in Columbus, Ohio. A study reported that remote classrooms with children 6–8 years old in Japan and Australia linked to a robot teacher resulted in much higher interaction versus a human teacher. Studies do show that children can learn from robots, particularly in the application area of robot language teaching. (Elbeck, 2016, p. 376)

> Preschool and elementary teachers who have incorporated robots in their classes have asserted that socialization between young children and robots is possible for extended periods of time and that humanoid robots can preserve long term relationships with humans. (Ioannou et al., 2015, p. 23)

> Research has shown that the intervention of a robot allows young children to become more motivated to learn, experience more social emotions during the learning process, and participate more frequently. Robots have been used to develop the vocabulary of infants 1.5–2 years of age to promote young children's language expressiveness during storytelling activity and to enrich storytelling with emotions that are transferred through the humanoid robot's gestures and posture. (Ioannou et al., 2015, p. 24)

"Robots have been used to extract secrets from children, related to abuses they might have experienced" (Ioannou et al., 2015, p. 24). Children are more trusting of robots versus humans. They feel as though the robot is their equal and possesses no threat.

> The research showed that children disclosed a secret to a robot easier than to an adult. More recently, studies have explored the humanoid robot as a learning tool. Studies show that robots help improve young children's reading better than other technologies, while it strengthens collaboration and promotes interactivity. (Ioannou et al., 2015, p. 24)

"Younger people reported more positive feelings (e.g., amused, pleasant, or relaxed) about domestic robots than did adults and elderly people. The younger people did not express any anxiety regarding the notion of a domestic robot" (Tung, 2016, p. 493).

Robots in Preschool Classes

Typically, teachers are using a robot called NAO in classrooms for preschoolers. NAO can be programmed to sit, get up, walk, dance, talk, and grasp objects, which immediately commands the attention of the child.

> Four preschoolers, 3–5 years of age, participated in the study for approximately one hour. NAO was placed in an indoor playground together with other toys (dolls, cars, bears, etc.). The children entered the playroom (all at the same time) and had a few minutes to explore and play around. A few minutes later, NAO stood up from his seated position, welcomed the children and introduced himself. NAO danced, walked, grasped toys and talked to the children. (Ioannou et al., 2015, p. 24)

This study, along with others, reveals that children are more accepting to robots compared to adults.

The video analysis showed that the children were comfortable with NAO, touched and explored him and communicated with him as if he were a peer (e.g., "Why don't you dance more?"). Also, the analysis revealed that the children were most interested in NAO when he moved and danced, whereas they lost interest during the storytelling activity (NAO telling a fairytale). During dancing NAO faced a technical problem and fell down which drew the children's further attention. In this case, children were compassionate and touched NAO to comfort him. One of the children kissed NAO on the head (twice); others gave him hugs and cuddling asking if he was crying and if he was hurt. It was evident that the children didn't see NAO as a toy, but rather as a peer. (Ioannou et al., 2015, p. 25)

MILESTONES

Despite some of the shortfalls of robust forecasts, the robotics field has grown consistently over the last decade, and there are predictions of impressive growth going forward.

A recent report for *Business Insider Intelligence* predicted the market growth for consumer and business robots to be $1.5 billion by 2019. This market is expected to grow at a compound annual growth rate of 17% until then, seven times faster than the manufacturing robot market. (Fassbender, 2015, p. 27)

A growth rate of 17 percent puts the consumer and business robot industry firmly in the top-ten growth rates in the United States (Biery, 2018). This fact alone should make academic leaders sit up and take notice. This industry will support strong workforce development for years to come.

CHALLENGES FACING THE INDUSTRY

It may seem as if the robot industry growth has been slow. In reality, the facts show that the prediction of robots taking over the world seems increasingly possible, as the industry has been growing steadily since the 1980s. However, there are challenges:

When a technology is first introduced, we may expect more than it can deliver. This period has been called the Age of Over-Expectation. Following is a period of disillusionment in which less is expected than the technology can actually deliver. This period is called the Time of Nightmare. Finally, reality sets in and we learn to expect only what the technology can deliver—the Age of Realism. The industrial robot has now reached this age of realism. (Hall, 2001, p. 8)

The researchers interviewed Tony Bailey from Research Robotics, Inc. Research Robotics is based in Boston and is best known for their collaborative robot, Baxter. A collaborative robot definition is set by ISO (International Standards Organization), meaning that the robot can be used anywhere without the need for a barrier or guard. The Baxter Robot has since been replaced by the Sawyer Robot, which has been hugely successful in an industrial setting. Mr. Bailey, who works in the research and education markets, delineated some of the difficulty of moving robots to the marketplace.

- Question: Where is the robotics field now?
- Answer: It's still at a juncture where robots are still too difficult for widespread deployment (T. Bailey, personal communication, June 12, 2018).
- Question: Sawyer is collaborative and sensor-driven. Is it ready to take over manufacturing?
- Answer: True, Sawyer is more collaborative and a smarter, more sensor-driven robot than its industrial counterparts, but it's not at a level of being entirely user-friendly to the point where it's a no-brainer decision for a small- to the mid-sized manufacturer. There's been a lot of progress in the collaborative robot world, but there still needs to be a lot of functionality built in to make these solutions easier (T. Bailey, personal communication, June 12, 2018).

Great strides are being made in the field of robotics, but the industry is very technical, and while improvements come every day, the field, despite being decades old, still needs to grow and mature.

OUTLOOK

Short Term (1–5 Years)

Personal robot deployment lags behind industrial robot deployments but are quickly surpassing industrial robot deployment in the marketplace.

> There is an international trend in robotics from industrial applications towards robots that play a role in personal life. The development of pet robots, toy robots, and other robots suggests a near-future scenario in which living with robots will be as habitual as living with TV, mobile phones, and the internet. (Coeckelbergh, 2009, p. 1)

An important point to understand is that both the industrial robot and the personal robot industries are growing. Furthermore, both industries are growing at a top-ten pace in the United States. "Semiconductor researcher Future Horizons in Kent, England, predicts that there will be 55.6 million robots in the world—many of them domestic robots—in a market worth $59.3 billion" (Edwards, 2004, p. 85).

The short-term future of robotics is promising for both industrial and personal robots. According to a Future Horizons report cited by *BusinessWeek*, "The electronics industry is on the cusp of a robotics wave, a period in which applications are aimed at human labor-saving and extending human skills" (Edwards, 2004, p. 85).

Mid-Term (5–10 Years)

The mid-term outlook for the robotics industry as a whole is very robust. Both the industrial segment and the personal segment of robotics will proliferate. Several strategies considered short-term are coming into play now that will have positive effects on the mid-term and subsequently the long-term outlook. "The Net strategy promises major improvements in every aspect of human endeavor. Making communication and information available to a broader community will make intelligent robots easier to conceive of, investigate, develop, produce and use" (Hall, 2001, p. 1).

Money, an apparent driver of the industry, is entering the marketplace, as well. "Jobo, 'The World's First Family Robot,' raised more than $2 million on the crowdfunding platform Indigogo, making it one of the most funded projects in the site's history" (Fassbender, 2015, p. 26). This influx of money bodes well for this nascent personal robot market.

Additionally, a recent report from *Business Insider Intelligence* predicted that market growth for consumer and business robots to be $1.5 billion by 2019. This market is expected to grow at a compound annual growth rate of 17 percent until then, seven times faster than the manufacturing robot market (Fassbender, 2015, p. 27). The mid-term and long-term industry outlook looks bullish.

Long Term (10–20 Years)

The timing is right for the massive growth taking place in the robotics industry, which is now two distinct sectors: industrial robotics and personal robotics.

> We would love to see social robotics go from being a far-fetched and foreign idea to a welcome addition to hectic 21st-century lives. Absolutely see robots becoming a more regular part of everyday life, Jibo and other robots are designed to assist, not replace human interaction. (Fassbender, 2015, p. 27)

More money is flowing into the industry, making the long-term forecast for robotics decidedly positive.

Aldebaran, part of the Softbank Robotic Holding Group, has sold 1,000 of its Pepper vision-guided humanoid robots within one minute of its initial launch. Alibaba Group Holding and Foxconn Technology have each invested $118 million for a combined 40 percent share of the SoftBank Robotic Holding Group. (Baron, 2015, p. 7)

Deals like the above are being reached and new money is entering the industry at increasing rates. This bodes well for the long-term outlook of the industry. An important point to understand is the geographical way in which these industries are taking shape. "Japan is the mecca of robotic pets as well as the first humanoid robots. Companies there are investing hundreds of millions of dollars to preserve their lead" (Edwards, 2004, p. 85). This means that the industry is still young and growing in the United States, and the industry has outstanding long-term prospects.

IMPACT ON COMMUNITY COLLEGES

The impact of these new industries on community colleges will be dramatic, not just in the short term, with increased demand for a workforce, but to support these new top-ten growth industries in the mid-term and the long term. New jobs and job functions will need to be taught to the future workers in these industries.

"Robots are taking over . . . literally. Technological advances creating 'disruptive innovations' across a host of industries are generating seismic shifts in the workforce and how workers can remain qualified and competitive in the job market" (Bryan, 2018, p. 1). A workforce is going to be needed to satisfy the growth of this industry, and the workforce has to have more than a high school diploma.

> Another factor impacting human workers is a dramatic swing in minimum education requirements of jobs because of the increased integration of technology. The National Skills Coalition recently highlighted that 35 years ago, only 28% of jobs required some type of college-level education and training. Today, 80% do. Half of those are middle skills jobs that require career specific certifications or associate degrees. (Bryan, 2018, p. 1)

It is understood that these skills will be taught in our higher education institutions. However, it is the nature of the job that should be addressed and analyzed, and training ideally should take place on the job.

> College is key, but "college" doesn't only mean "university." According to the National Center for Education Statistics, 69% of high school seniors go straight into college after graduation, which is good. However, less than a third

of them are choosing the two-year colleges whose programs align education to faster employment in high-demand middle-skill jobs. (Bryan, 2018, p. 1)

This fact represents a tremendous opportunity for community colleges and an opportunity that should be exploited in the short term and planned for in the long term. Workers will need certificates to gain employment in these new industries, and perhaps just as critical are other workers who are working in less fulfilling sectors who will want the opportunity to venture into these fast-growth industries. A lot of these workers cannot take four years off to obtain a credential. These workers need to work now for myriad reasons.

> This is important because the majority of college students are also working full- or part-time jobs. In fact, lack of funds and the need to work are two of the top reasons students don't graduate. Having a credential, certificate or two-year degree puts them in a position to earn more with the time they have and pave the way to both completion and careers. (Bryan, 2018, p. 2)

As the industry matures and grows, new skills must be learned, and the employees of these industries are going to have to return and take classes to learn and develop these new skills, creating an even more significant opportunity for colleges.

IMPACT ON UNIVERSITIES

There is a great deal of room for university training in these money-laden industries, as well.

> We have to understand that education is not a destination. It's part of the journey toward a career. That journey can have multiple finish lines, each one carrying with it increased earning power and the skills to use the technology we have, or to create our own disruptive innovations that change the future of work. Along the way we need to develop the critical thinking, complex problem solving, written and oral communication, and applied knowledge skills that 75% of New Mexico's employers want, and robots simply cannot provide. (Bryan, 2018, p. 2)

Some of these needed skills cannot be garnered in the local community college, as community colleges and universities differ in purpose. Programs of study need to be formulated for both categories of institution.

The researchers interviewed Dr. Tamara Lorenz, an assistant professor at the University of Cincinnati. Dr. Lorenz is a psychologist with a master's degree in mechanical engineering. The doctor studies human/robot interactions. The interview covered a great deal, ending up on the subject of what it might take to work in this budding industry.

- Question: What are these robotic companies asking for, what education are they requiring?
- Answer: You know, they approach me if they need some high-level skill set. They don't come to me and tell me: I need welders (T. Lorenz, personal communication, June 21, 2018).
- Question: What are the companies asking for, and do you teach the skills they are looking for here in your labs?
- Answer: They tell me, "I need more programmers," or, "We need more control engineers." Stuff like that, right? But mostly, industry approaches me for human-robot interaction, because that's my expertise. I'm actually not teaching the robot control. I'm teaching the intersection of how do robots have to act and look like and be designed, so that humans can intuitively and safely interact with them (T. Lorenz, personal communication, June 21, 2018).
- Question: So these companies are looking for specific types of engineers?
- Answer: I mean, the interesting thing about robotics, and the challenge, the big challenge is that it's not enough. If you have a mechanical engineering degree purely, it's not enough for robotics (T. Lorenz, personal communication, June 21, 2018).
- Question: So, you need a broader education?
- Answer: So, it's all about interdisciplinary education, I would say. You need to tackle other fields. You need to be open for other fields, at least if you're a mechanical engineer, at least be open for electrical engineering, right? Be open for computer science, machine learning. These kind of things. And if you're a little more thriving, then be open for really other disciplines like psychology, social science, linguistics. Because all of that is important. So I would say if you're interested in creating a new program for educating roboticists, let them explore a little more than just the mechanics. That will give them a skill set that distinguishes them from others (T. Lorenz, personal communication, June 21, 2018).

It is apparent that there is a need for a ready workforce with varying levels of education. More importantly, there exists the opportunity for new interdisciplinary programs designed to meet the needs of the robotics industry. There are opportunities for both higher education institutions and the students they serve.

ADVICE TO ADMINISTRATORS ON HIGHER EDUCATION

Leaders must garner the facts and the data available to make decisions. In this case, the facts and data show that the robotics industry is expanding at near record growth rates, currently, top-ten in growth rate in the United States, for the foreseeable future (Biery, 2018). This vital information, at the very least, should cause the opening of discussions on what institutions may do to better serve this industry in both the short term and the long term. Most colleges and universities are behind the curve when looking at the robotics industry.

Some institutions have robotics programs, but the industry growth rates are eclipsing these institutions' ability to produce the necessary workforce and a workforce with the skills required by the manufacturers. In the short term, these problems must be solved and in the long term, plans must be made to create programs that produce the types of workers these companies require to continue to grow the industry and meet the analyst's projections.

CONCLUSION

The robotics field is growing larger in both size (more revenue) and scope (more uses for robots). The growth has been increasing at an exponential rate, and projections show that this growth is expected to continue for many years.

The industries, both commercial and personal, are witnessing a shortage of available workers at differing skill levels. While some colleges and universities are training students to enter these fields, the collective output of the colleges and universities is not enough to satisfy the needs of the industry. The statistics show that the industry is vibrant and will remain so for the long term; therefore it is necessary to add additional programs at more institutions to supply the required workforce.

This is an opportunity to create a healthy education program that serves both the needs of the community and society at large. It is critical for the industry to have the workforce available to grow and prosper. The proximate result of creating programs to educate students to fill these vital jobs is that both the academic institutions and the industries will thrive. This is an incredible opportunity to show not only the industry, but society as a whole, the real value of higher education.

CHAPTER SUMMARY

- Some researchers predict a loss of 50 percent of U.S. jobs to robots.
- Past predictions of job loss have been incorrect.
- New jobs may replace current jobs.
- Robots are being developed for use in human rehabilitation.
- Will humans be willing to interact with robots?

- With all the menial tasks that robots can provide, not all Americans are comfortable with robots coming into their homes providing these services.
- In other countries and in some parts of the United States, robots are used in classrooms to assist teachers with students.
- Research has shown that the intervention of a robot allows young children to become more motivated to learn, experience more social emotions during the learning process, and participate more frequently.
- Children appear to be more accepting of robots than are adults.
- Despite some of the shortfalls of robust forecasts, the robotics field has grown consistently over the last decade, and there are predictions of impressive growth going forward.
- It may seem as if the robot industry growth has been slow; in reality, the facts show the prediction of robots taking over the world seems increasingly possible, as the industry has been growing steadily since the 1980s.
- Personal robot deployment lags behind industrial robot deployments but is quickly surpassing industrial robot deployment in the marketplace.
- The short-term future of robotics is promising for both industrial and personal robots. In the next five to ten years, both industrial segments and personal segments of robots will proliferate.
- The timing is right for massive growth to take place in the robotics industry during the ten-to-twenty-year period.
- More money is flowing into the industry, making the long-term forecast for robotics decidedly positive.
- The impact of robotics on community colleges will be dramatic.
- New jobs and job functions will need to be taught to future workers in these industries.
- Workers will need certificates to gain employment in these new industries, and perhaps just as critical is that the other workers who are working in less-fulfilling sectors will want the opportunity to venture into these faster-growth industries.
- And as the industry matures and grows, new skills must be learned by the employees of the industries involved; they are going to have to return and take classes to learn and develop these new skills, creating an even more significant opportunity for colleges.
- Administrators in higher education must follow the facts and data that show the robotics industry is expanding at near-record rates.
- Some institutions have robotic programs, but the industry growth rates are eclipsing the institution's ability to produce the necessary workforce with the skills required by manufacturers.
- It is critical that the industry have the workforce available to grow and prosper.
- The proximate result of creating programs to educate students to fill these vital jobs is that both academic institutions and industry will thrive.

REFERENCES

(2015, October). Humanoid personal robot sells rapidly. *Vision Systems Design, 20*(9), 7.
Are Robots the Next Eldercare Trend? (2018). *Journal of Financial Planning, 31*(1), 16–18.
Baron, N. S. (2015). Shall We Talk? Conversing with Humans and Robots. *Information Society, 31*(3), 257–64.
Biery, M. E. (2018, May 13). These 10 industries are growing the fastest in the U.S. *Forbes.* Retrieved from https://www.forbes.com/sites/sageworks/2018/05/13/10-fastest-growing-industries-u-s/#76e48ba3907f.
Bryan, T. (2018, March 28). Staying ahead of the robot apocalypse. *Sun-News.* Retrieved from https://www.icsun-news.com/story/money/business/2018/03/28/staying-ahead-robot-apocalypse/464531002.
Coeckelbergh, M. (2009). Personal robots, appearance, and human good: A methodological reflection on roboethics. Retrieved from https://link.springer.com/article/10.1007/s12369-009-0026-2.
Edwards, C. (2004, July 19). Ready to buy a home robot. *BusinessWeek*, 84–90.
Elbeck, M. (2016). Humanoid Robots as a Paradigm Shift for Marketing Education—Embrace or Resist? *Society for Marketing Advances Proceedings*, 375–82.
Fassbender, M. (2015, January/February). Designing a personal robot. *Product Design & Development, 70*(1), 26–27.
Ford, M. (2015). *Rise of the robots: Technology and the threat of a jobless future.* New York: Basic Books.
Hall, E. L. (2001). *Intelligent robot trends and predictions for the .net future* [White paper]. Retrieved from https://doi.org/10.1117/12.444228.
Ioannou, A. A., Andreou, E., & Christofi, M. (2015). Pre-schoolers' Interest and Caring Behaviour Around a Humanoid Robot. *Techtrends: Linking Research & Practice to Improve Learning, 59*(2), 23–26.
Tung, F. (2016). Child Perception of Humanoid Robot Appearance and Behavior. *International Journal of Human-Computer Interaction, 32*(6), 493–502.

Chapter Five

Human Genome

Ghada Gouda and Angelo Markantonakis

Since the discovery of the DNA molecular structure in 1953, by James Watson and Francis Crick, scientists have been using this marked milestone to make significant changes to science. Since that discovery point to the information age of modern biology, in which technological improvements have created limitless scientific breakthroughs, the human genome has been researched.

THE HUMAN GENOME PROJECT

The Human Genome Project (HGP) is discussed within a linear progression of short-term, mid-term, and long-term changes. "Initially, the HGP set out to determine a human genetic map, then a physical map of human genome, and finally the sequence map" (Hood & Rowen, 2013, p. 2). Over time, academic institutions have developed curriculum programs within the field to mimic topics of HGP.

How these changes will affect community colleges and senior institutions is discussed. Advice for both administrators within academic institutions and future students is given. Interviews and campus visits with academic institutions, senior level educators, and programs within the field of human genome have been conducted and are discussed.

HGP has taken incremental steps within genome sequencing over time. Many educational institutions work closely with smaller genomes in attempts to relate to the human genome.

> In our neurobiology lab we use *C. elegans*. It is a microscopic, non-parasitic, transparent soil nematode that is one of the best characterized genetic model organisms. The vast genetic, genomic and anatomical resources available in this organism and the world-wide network of scientists that use this animal

make it a very powerful model to study the nervous system. What we hope is that what we learn in the worm, can be studied in a mammal, specifically looking at brain connections and how neurons find other neurons. (R. El Bejjani, personal communication, June 29, 2018)

The model used at Davidson College parallels with the historical approach of using smaller genome sequencing.

As a key component of the HGP, it was wisely decided to sequence the smaller genomes of significant experimental model organisms of yeast, worm, fruit fly, and arabidopsis thaliana, a small flowering plant, before taking on the far more challenging human genome. (Hood & Rowen, 2013, p. 2)

Ultimately, with the goal of correlating connectivity of various genome sequences, such as the worm mentioned above, and the human genome research projects are conducted. The constant theme in education is to conduct these research projects toward neuron connections. These projects assist in teaching students about new technology. They follow a pattern with projects starting with smaller genomes before working with the human genome.

Medical Transformation

Medical genomics is starting to transform patient care. "The genome sequences of microbes, plants and animals have revolutionized many fields of science, including microbiology, virology, infectious disease and plant biology. Moreover, deeper knowledge of human sequence variation has begun to alter the practice of medicine" (Hood & Rowen, 2013, p.1). With more effort being placed on addressing medical issues and drug metabolism, the level of genotype, rather than an individual person, will transform patient care, communication, and the speed of diagnostic capabilities within health care.

CRISPR/Cas9

New advanced technologies in Clustered Regularly Interspaced Short Palindromic Repeats (CRISPR), along with the enzyme Cas9, CRISPR/Cas9, is utilized to alter DNA. CRISPR-Cas9 makes altering sequences of DNA strands occur in an expedited manner. Both technologies are changing the pace of scientific research. Universities will be a cornerstone in developing human genome science. Community colleges will prepare an employable workforce in the future to work in the genome science field.

HUMAN GENOME OPPORTUNITIES IN HIGHER EDUCATION AT PRESENT

Supporting the students who are interested in studying genomes and genetics comes through providing them with internships, scholarships, grants, and opportunities to learn. Further support for students comes in the forms of exposing them to the technology through new educational programs and guiding students through advising.

Dr. Craig Venter, who started his undergraduate education at a community college in California, supports the community college students in his Institute by assisting them to accelerate their education and experience. "The Genomics Scholars Program (GSP) is a long-term internship designed to help community college students with a science focus transition to four-year colleges. GSP began in 2014" and ended in the summer of 2018 (Genomics Scholars Program, n.d., reviewed).

Grants

Grant opportunities focus on helping students conduct collaborative genomics research with faculty through the Davidson Research Initiative. The grant has been active since 2007. The emphasis is for students to ascertain ownership of their research and rejuvenate faculty as students view genomic research through a fresh lens (Davidson Research Initative, n.d.). Similar grant programs for scientific research opportunities are available, hoping for breakthroughs that will bring future government funding.

Internships and Scholarships

Internship and scholarship opportunities illustrate the methods in which educational institutions are exposing students to program opportunities. In the process of weaving in a student's interests, they can conduct scientific research projects. These types of educational opportunities create a foundation for students in a safe, inquisitive environment, allowing for personal growth and the prospect of publishing their findings.

CRISPR/Cas9 Technology

Many books and research papers discuss how CRISPR/Cas9 started and how it has made a huge impact in science. Kruminis-Kaszkiel et al. (2018) explained how the first CRISPR loci was discovered in 1987 by identifying a mysterious DNA sequence in *Escherichia coli*. Panoutsos (2016) discussed the huge leap CRISPR/Cas9 made to research in different fields such as human reproduction, health, and drugs.

"New world is emerging from its egg, the surface of gene-editing and modification techniques cracks open and out comes ... CRISPR! Is this new power-of-god the new progressive front of technology, is it blasphemy or is it just senseless and unwise tomfoolery?" (Panoutsos, 2016, p. 112). This improvement in quickly assessing DNA has revolutionized scientific processes and discoveries.

CRISPR/Cas9 technology has proven to assist in understanding and treating many health-related conditions; however, it is still imperfect and has some issues. Kruminis-Kaszkiel et al. (2018) explained some limitations of the CRISPR/Cas9 system, such as DNA sequencing. Sequences could be off-target, causing incorrect or undesirable mutations (Hood & Rowen, 2013).

Community colleges and universities are exposing their students to CRISPR/Cas9 technology, as it is one of the current and future foundations that are applicable to human genome sciences. Higher education institutions are preparing students to contribute to the future improvement of genome science.

Short Term (1–5 Years)

Within the next five years there will be a need to incorporate exposure of students earlier to genomic research. An innovative program, developed at the Gene Editing Institute, Christiana Care's Helen F. Graham Cancer Center & Research Institute, in a partnership with Delaware Community College, is aimed to give a learning experience to high school students with the goal of recruiting those who are interested in studying gene science.

Together the institutions are showcasing a unique, hands-on experience in gene editing. "The program expands on a National Science Foundation grant in which the Gene Editing Institute partners with Delaware Technical Community College to provide curriculum to educate future research lab workers"(CRISPR in High School, n.d., reviewed). This exposure will allow younger generations of students to get involved in ways that will shape their educational journeys.

Ethical Considerations

The alteration of genes leads genomics down a critical ethical path. An example of this is the concept of designer babies through gene manipulation, which would incorporate the concepts of having children with specific characteristics predetermined. "The HGP benefited biology and medicine by creating a sequence of the human genome; sequencing model organisms; developing high-throughput sequencing technologies; and examining the ethical and social issues implicit in such technologies" (Hood & Rowen, 2013, p. 4).

Higher education institutions will need to create policies and procedures that align with the needed framework for understanding the interpretations of genomics and gene-related research ethics. Health-care and scientific programs within education will need to specifically align their curricula with the pace of CRISPR/Cas9 technology, as medical diagnostic capabilities are quickly changing.

"Several genomic studies have tried to identify patients with the greatest likelihood of receiving short-term benefits from whole-genome sequencing tests, specifically in the areas of diagnosis and management" (Pasic et al., 2013, p. 160). Within a brief period of time, educational programs such as nursing, radiological technology, lab technicians, and biotechnology will need to educate students on the advanced testing being conducted on patients.

Mid-Term (5–10 Years)

The need to integrate genetic technology into the framework of evidence-based DNA research will be paramount to the success of genome science. Genomic research provides a new realm of possibilities to higher education. "Many of the greatest and most revolutionary ideas, from moon rockets to invisibility, have been anticipated by myth, legend, and, of course, science fiction. This is also true of our efforts to use our understanding of the software of life" (Venter, 2014, p. 160).

The implications of digitizing DNA research with the ideals of human software will be an important phase of changes for human genome science. Taking this a step further is an example illustrated by Venter: "With *Haemophilus* influenzae we had transformed the double helix of biology into the digital world of computer, but the fun was only now beginning" (Venter, 2014, p. 52). Transforming DNA research into technological capabilities will allow for global involvement. This can also connect to sharing larger amounts of information.

Many of the results of genomic research are housed in various databases. The need to create an integrated system of this information is becoming evident. "Moreover, now becoming available are several national and international public databases that integrate different levels of molecular high-throughput analyses to draw meaningful 'actionable' conclusions that can help in managing patients" (Pasic et al., 2013, p. 160).

There will be increased opportunities for advancement in drugs, vaccines, treatments, and diagnostic measures. Higher education institutions will need to have the ability to allow students to review tangible material for scientific research. Access to the resources and databases that can display information of past and current data will have a huge impact on genome science. The unification of research that is occurring with fresh sets of eager scientists could be a limitless mid-term change.

Higher education institutions will need to prepare for the employment needs of genome technology companies who are in need of trained database managers and technicians. In addition, the health-care and technology programs will need to be ready to add in employability skills that incorporate health-care sciences and information technology. "Furthermore, a large database can be created with complete profiles from more individuals with different types of diseases. Such a database may be available in the diagnosis, monitoring, and treatment of diseases" (Pasic et al., 2013, p. 161).

Long Term (10–20 Years)

Three main gene-editing tools are currently utilized in genome research: CRISPR/Cas9 as mentioned above, Transcription Activator-Like Effector Nuclease (TALEN), and Zinc Finger Nuclease (ZFN). There will always be innovations to these tools and their usage. TALEN and ZFN are used often and are "two of the most powerful tools helping research do enormous progress in the field of biological research" (Panoutsos, 2016, p. 356).

Continuous improvement and troubleshooting the limitations of these scientific tools will change the long-term approaches to research within genome science. Possible merging of technologies may also occur in areas such as Synthetic Genomics, Inc. (SGI). With the ability to take digital DNA code and rebuild the sequence in a laboratory, a watchful eye will need to be placed on the evolution of editing tools.

The impact on consumerism has yet to be mentioned in how patients, doctors, and the service industries will work toward redefining health care. The review of an individual's genome sequence could eventually lead to the doctor's specific choices for their therapeutic needs.

> We predict that individual genome sequences will soon play a larger role in medical practice. In the ideal scenario, patients or consumers will use the information to improve their own healthcare by taking advantage of prevention or therapeutic strategies that are known to be appropriate for real or potential medical conditions suggested by their individual genome sequence. Physicians will need to educate themselves on how best to advise patients who bring consumer genetic data to their appointments, which may well be a common occurrence in a few years. (Hood & Rowen, 2013, p. 5)

There will be a need for strong collaborative approaches and strategic planning processes to prepare for the long-term effects of how health-care information, transactions, and services are performed. "Current examples of research illustrate the ability to edit genes, slow the spread of cancer cells, block cancer mutations, correct mutations, cure genetic defects, and create biological computers inside living cells called transcriptors" (News Center, n.d.).

As sequencing technology progresses, so will gene-editing capabilities. "Newer generations of DNA sequencing platforms will be introduced that will transform how we gather genome information. Third-generation sequencing will employ nanopores or nanochannels, utilize electronic signals, and sequence single DNA molecules for read lengths of 10,000 to 100,000 bases" (Hood & Rowen, 2013, p. 7). Newer generations of gene editing will spearhead changes in sequencing and research initiatives.

EFFECTS ON COMMUNITY COLLEGES AND UNIVERSITIES

Alec Ross states best what future community colleges and universities must prepare for. "In the years ahead, we will live in a world where we'll be able to target cancer cells with true precision, breathe air out of lungs transplanted from farm animals, and deliver medical treatment from the best hospitals in the world to the poorest most remote corners of the earth" (Ross, 2016, p. 47). All areas of curriculum programs within an academic institution will feel the ripple of changes within human genome science. Below are various areas that will directly impact academic institutions.

Genomic Medicine

The National Human Genome Research Institute (NHGRI) defines genomic medicine as "an emerging medical discipline that involves using genomic information about an individual as part of their clinical care (e.g., for diagnostic or therapeutic decision-making) and the health outcomes and policy implications of that clinical use" (*What Is Genomic Medicine?*, n.d.).

Areas such as oncology are incorporating genomics for diagnostic markers leading to tailored treatment approaches.

Genomic medicine can range from DNA sequencing and new drug treatments to rejected transplant organs, cancer cell studies, and newborn screening searching for mutations (*What Is Genomic Medicine?*, n.d.). Such studies will create the need for new academic programs in biotechnologies. Further, there will be the need to develop the workforce with capable clinical technicians.

Pharmacy, Pharmacogenomics, and Blood Diagnostics

The drug industry will change as pharmacies align with genetic findings. Pharmacogenomics is known as a treatment specific to genetic review findings.

> Tailored treatment—it's now understood that some of the variability in how people respond to medications is explained by the way their bodies interact with drugs. The field of pharmacogenomics seeks to understand these differ-

ences. For some medications, identifying individual gene differences can help customize both the selection of medications and dosing for the best response. (Goodman et al., 2013, p. 1544)

An individual's genetic profile will be able to create treatment plans that will match their specific patient biological, physiological, and psychological needs.

There will be major economic benefits of pharmacogenomics. This could impact businesses, individual patients, and health care on many levels.

> The approximately 1000 deaths that result make adverse drug reactions the fourth leading cause of death: Moreover, the estimated annual cost of drug-related morbidity and mortality in the US is >$76 billion. Added to this is the waste of medications administered to the patients who do not respond. On average, a given medication will have a therapeutic effect in only 25% to 60% of patients. (Pasic et al., 2013, p. 162)

The long-term implications of collecting the data created by pharmacogenomics will also correlate with the research conducted relative to the human genome. The potential to merge drug databases with DNA research is possible.

Technology is creating opportunities to review DNA at a rapid pace. "We anticipate that we will soon be able to quantify thousands of proteins and assess the function or disease of many organs simply by using a drop of blood" (Pasic et al., 2013, p. 162). This process could save time and money, and improve services to consumers and stakeholders.

Legal and Ethical Issues

The ownership of data, policies, procedures, and ethical ramifications will be tested on all human genome science concepts. The potential merging of large databases, and the effects of so much knowledge, will open new terrains. The information received from conducted research will create new theoretical understandings. There will be a need for clear guidance to travel such uncharted territories, not only with science, but with laws and regulations.

> The issue of securing these large amounts of data is also a concern. Patent issues (Who owns the genes?) is another ongoing debate in the scientific community. Finally, direct-to-consumer genetic testing should be evaluated cautiously in terms of its reliability and the impact of these tests on the public. In addition, providing these tests to the public must be regulated. (Pasic et al., 2013, p. 165)

Academic institutions must collaborate with policymakers and legal advisors and make sure their information is technologically secure. A safe environment will be needed to guide students through a new arena of law, ethics, and research methods.

FUTURE JOBS

There are some promising jobs related to the study of genes. Forensic science technician is one example of a favorable job with a bright future. Another example would be research assistants as a future job opportunity accepting entry-level candidates. Academic institutions will need to collaborate with employers in their communities to establish the skill sets needed by students.

As mentioned above, within short-term change, it is imperative that youth be exposed to concepts that will expand their horizons within the human genome employment potential. "Given that the current generation of high school students will come of age in an era when personal genetic information is becoming increasingly used in healthcare, ensuring students understand the genetic concepts necessary to make informed medical decisions is of vital importance" (Pasic et al., 2013, p. 163). The future is promising for employment within the lab technician, research assistant, and technological realms.

Time

With new laws, ethical questions, and policies on the horizon, the concept of time has never been more in the spotlight. Considering that academic institutions operate under the guise of some form of an accrediting body such as the Southern Association of Colleges and Schools Commission on Colleges (SACS/COC), strict timelines, procedures, guidelines, and auditing processes are always imminent. The addition of scientific inquiry could make the pace of progression glacial. "It has often been estimated that it takes, on average, 17 years to translate a novel research finding into routine clinical practice" (*What Is Genomic Medicine?*, n.d.). With future collaborations, the use of public databases, and review processes, research could expedite the process.

Challenges

Innovative technology assists in opening new doors for new careers. Technology itself may be a challenge. Machines may compete in taking some positions and career opportunities from the human being in the information age and beyond. "Computers are becoming very proficient at acquiring skills, especially when a large amount of training data is available. Entry-level jobs, in particular, are likely to be heavily affected, and there is an evidence that this may already be occurring" (Ford, 2016, p. xv).

Academic institutions must keep their programs current and up-to-date on technological changes. Updates and alignments of curriculum and new technologies must be ever-evolving. Policies, procedures, and updated technology will need to be aligned with government, policymaking, and research guidelines.

ADVICE TO ADMINISTRATORS OF COMMUNITY COLLEGES AND UNIVERSITIES

Administrators and faculty will need to stay open-minded. As whenever anything is new, there will be learning opportunities, from budgetary expenses to collaboration with the wide variety of stakeholders. Decisions made regarding human genome programs and courses will need to be timely and related to the mission of the communities being served.

> One of the trickiest parts is that budgets tend not to be nimble, and learning leaders need the ability to be flexible and to experiment. In my experience, learning leaders are often forced into "all or nothing" investment choices. They have a choice between investing in enterprise-wide systems with a multi-year commitment and a lot of risk, or not changing anything, and the latter offers more certainty and security. Learning leaders need to be able to try different programs and methods on different audiences within an enterprise to test and measure the product/market fit; how well a specific program fits their enterprise. (Ross, 2017)

Administrators and faculty will need to engage the local community. There is a need to ensure a successful understanding of the offerings available at academic institutions relative to human genome sciences. There will also be a strong need to integrate these basic human genome concepts into the K–12 educational partners.

Faculty

Faculty will need to create opportunities for students to simplify and utilize critical thinking practices to delve into the potential topics within human genome science. "Find ways to immerse students in experiences, and other interactions. Give them opportunities to take personal ownership of their work" (R. El Bejjani, personal communication, June 29, 2018). Research findings generated by students at academic institutions could create future opportunities for funding larger projects.

Funding

Funding will be a key component to the opportunities generated for human genome research, programs, and science at educational institutions.

> We apply for external funds and have competitive grants for faculty. The Davidson research initiative has impacted so many students in such a positive manner. Our student projects could be applications as student work to the government, to work toward funding to find out the answers to these questions. External funds could be for additional work to expand our capabilities. We have limited resources, we maximize the resources we have to get as much as we can for our students. (R. El Bejjani, personal communication, June 29, 2018)

Resources

New technology, additional faculty, support staff, and resources could all be impacted with established funding sources. The learning experience of the student can also be enriched by continuous improvements of labs, curriculum, and learning resources. If updates and improvements do not occur, it could be detrimental to a program's success. Preparing students for the workforce could also create opportunities for future alumni donations and increased employment success.

Learning Leadership

A culture of learning will be needed for administrators and faculty. The atmosphere should offer motivation for the entire campus to engage in inquiry. Leadership will set the tone and the example for a campus culture of lifelong learning.

> Millennials make up an ever-larger and more senior part of our workforces; the way they learn and work will only grow in importance. . . . Learning leaders need to be intellectually omnivorous, taking in information from wildly varying sources. We need to be interdisciplinary learners ourselves if we expect to be good stewards of the learning environments in our organizations. (Ross, 2017)

Leadership will need to encourage teams and divisions of the academic institutions to initiate and motivate continuous educational developments. These practices will keep the learning atmosphere healthy. Allowing faculty to be members of local, regional, and international human genome research organizations will serve as a motivator for the faculty, students, and academic institution.

Collaboration, Bridging, and Training

Administrators and faculty will need to collaborate with the community, resources, stakeholders, and local employers. These partnerships will be essential to program success. "In the era of personalized genomics, it is important to emphasize the concept of collaboration rather than competition" (Pasic et al., 2013, p. 163). An example of an educational partnership under this approach is demonstrated between two colleges, one in Maryland and the other in California.

According to J. Craig Venter Institute Website (n.d.), The Genome Scholars Program offered by the J. Craig Venter Institute is an example of a partnership between the Institute and community colleges, including Montgomery College (Maryland) and MiraCosta College (California). The partnership assists the students after completing the program to continue their education in an accredited four-year academic institution in a STEM major.

Academic institutions will need to understand the importance of training programs in preparing successful workforce strategies for employers.

> Equally important is the need to train the new generation of clinicians and laboratory scientists to understand the different dimensions of these evolving applications. Training programs, such as TRIG (Training Residents in Genomics) curriculum (http://www.pathoogytraining.org), have already been established. Studies have suggested that the "genetic literacy" of the general public is inadequate to prepare citizens for this unprecedented access to genomic information. (Pasic et al., 2013, p. 163)

Training programs can take the form of integrated training during the workday in the form of professional development. Internships are another method of training that may give an opportunity for interns to gain full-time employment.

ADVICE TO STUDENTS IN COMMUNITY COLLEGES AND UNIVERSITIES

Recently, the needed skill sets for future students across all career and technical education curriculums were established for Perkins-related funding. The Perkins Act is a federal funding source "for the improvement of secondary and postsecondary career and technical education programs across the nation. The purpose of the Act is to develop more fully the academic, career, and technical skills of secondary and postsecondary students who elect to enroll in career and technical education programs" (*Legislation about Perkins*, n.d.).

A specific list highlights the broad skills that will help workers adapt to the changing career landscape for the twenty-first century. In no particular order, they are:

- Sense-making: the ability to determine the deeper meaning or significance of what is being expressed.

- Social intelligence: the ability to connect to others in a deep and direct way, to sense and stimulate reactions and desired interactions.
- Novel and adaptive thinking: proficiency at thinking and coming up with solutions and responses beyond that which is rote or rule-based.
- Cross-cultural competence: the ability to operate in different cultural settings.
- Computational thinking: the ability to translate vast amounts of data into abstract concepts and to understand data-based reasoning.
- New-media literacy: the ability to critically assess and develop content that uses new media forms and to leverage these media for persuasive communication.
- Transdisciplinary: literacy in and ability to understand concepts across multiple disciplines.
- Design mind-set: the ability to represent and develop tasks and work processes for desired outcomes.
- Cognitive load management: the ability to discriminate and filter information for importance and to understand how to maximize cognitive functioning using a variety of tools and techniques.
- Virtual collaboration: the ability to work productively, drive engagement, and demonstrate presence as a member of a virtual team (PCRN: Perkins Act).

Though these Perkins Act skill sets are established, future students must add to the conversation of needed skill sets as technological advances can alter and redefine the current list.

Dr. Rachid El Bejjani of Davidson College in North Carolina echoes many of the skill sets described for community college students as detailed above.

> This program offers a foundation for students to contribute to the field. They have an opportunity to get exposure by being involved in regional, national, and international conferences. They need to learn how to share their work to both layman and experts in the field, and learn how to conduct the communication of science. They get real hands-on research that they can take ownership of. None of the skills are lost such as critical thinking, writing, and troubleshooting. (R. El Bejjani, personal communication, June 29, 2018)

Taking the student perspective a step further, Dr. Bejjani describes the need for students to get comfortable being uncomfortable, and staying inquisitive about their interests. "As students, my advice would be to take the time to get comfortable with a lab. If possible, if you have an opportunity to meet with others who have been in the labs, learn from one another. Start having these interactions" (R. El Bejjani, personal communication, June 29, 2018). A combination of skills and exposure will benefit future students interested in human genome education and careers the most.

CONCLUSION

Human genomics will impact science, technology, and academic institutions. It is clear that human genomics will alter medicine, employment, and ethical boundaries. Technology will be crucial to these changes. "The merging of technology and genomics is not far off. A mobile phone cannot sequence someone's genome yet, but it can be used to take a blood sample and transmit the data to a lab on the other side of the world" (Ross, 2017, p. 70). HGP has impacted higher education, and it will impact curriculum for many years.

The HGP has affected the future of medical diagnostics, and pharmaceutical options for patients, and employment opportunities for students. Genomics will play a pivotal role in health care and education. "Genomics will become a trillion-dollar industry, extending lives and nearly eliminating diseases that kill hundreds of thousands of people a year today" (Ross, 2016, p. 75).

Community colleges and universities will need to redefine local partnerships, business resources, and current employment options for students. The changes within HGP will be closely linked to how academic institutions serve their communities.

CHAPTER SUMMARY

- The human genome project has taken incremental steps with genome sequencing over time.
- Medical genomics is starting to transform patient care.
- CRISPR/Cas9 is used to alter DNA.
- Universities will become a cornerstone in genome science development.
- Community colleges will prepare a suitable workforce for future development.
- Grant opportunities are the main focus for students attempting to conduct collaborative economic research.
- CRISPR/Cas9 technology, which can be used to quickly assess DNA, has revolutionized scientific processes and discoveries.
- Within the next five years, there will be a need to incorporate exposure of students earlier to the genomic research.
- The alteration of genes leads genomics down a critical, ethical path.
- Higher education institutions will need to create policies and procedures that align with the needed framework for understanding the interpretations of genomics and gene-related research ethics.
- Many of the results of genomic research are housed in various databases.
- There will be increased opportunities for advancement in drugs, vaccines, treatments, and diagnostic measures.

- Higher education institutions will need to prepare for the employment needs of the medical industry.
- With the ability to take digital DNA code and rebuild the sequence in a laboratory, a watchful eye will need to be placed on the evolution of editing tools.
- As sequencing technology progresses, so will gene-editing capabilities.
- There will be the need to develop the workforce of capable clinical technicians.
- The long-term implications of collecting the data created by pharmacogenomics will be integrated with the research conducted relative to the human genome.
- The ownership of data, policy, procedures, and ethical ramifications will be tested in all genome science concepts.
- There will be a need for clear guidance to travel into the uncharted territories, not only with science, but with laws and regulations.
- There are some promising jobs related to the study of genes, such as that of a forensic science technician, a research assistant, and other jobs not yet determined.
- Innovative technology assists in opening new doors for new careers.
- Academic institutions must keep their programs current and up-to-date on technological changes.
- Administrators and faculty will need to stay open-minded, as when anything is new, there will be learning opportunities.
- Faculty will need to create opportunities for students to simplify and utilize critical-thinking practices to delve into the potential topics within genome science.
- Funding will be a key component to the opportunities generated for genome research, programs, and science at higher education institutions.
- A culture of learning will be needed for administrators and faculty.
- Leadership will need to encourage teams in divisions of academic institutions to initiate and motivate continuous educational learning.
- Academic institutions will need to understand the importance of training programs and preparing successful workforce strategies for employers.
- A specific list of broad skills will help workers adapt to the changing career landscape for the twenty-first century.
- Those skills include sense-making, social intelligence, novel and adaptive thinking, cross-cultural competence, computational thinking, new media literacy, transit disciplinary, design mind-set, cognitive load management, and virtual collaboration.
- Human genomics will impact science, technology, and academic institutions.

REFERENCES

Alec Ross on the Future of Learning. (2017, February 23). Retrieved from http://www.clomedia.com/2017/02/23/alec-ross-future-of-learning/.
CRISPR in high school? Delaware students get hands-on gene editing training. (n.d.). Retrieved from https://news.christianacare.org/2018/02/high-school-students-acquire-hands-on-experience-in-gene-editing/.
Davidson Research Initiative. (n.d.). Retrieved from https://www.davidson.edu/academics/research/davidson-research-initiative.
Ford, M. (2016). *Rise of the robots: Technology and the threat of a jobless future*. New York: Basic Books.
Genomics Scholars Program. (n.d.). Retrieved from https://www.jcvi.org/genomics-scholars-program.
Goodman, D. M., Lynm, C., & Livingston, E. H. (2013). Genomic Medicine. *Jama, 309*(14), 1544. doi:10.1001/jama.2013.1927.
Hood, L., & Rowen, L. (2013). Retrieved from https://www.ncbi.nlm.nih.gov/pmc/articles/PMC4066586/.
J. Craig Venter Institute Website. www.jvci.org/genomics-scholars-institute.
Kruminis-Kaszkiel, E., Juranek, J., Maksymowicz, W., & Wojtkiewicz, J. (2018, March). Retrieved from https://www.ncbi.nlm.nih.gov/pmc/articles/PMC5877767/.
Legislation about Perkins. Retrieved from https://cte.ed.gov/legislation/about-perkins-iv.
News Center. (n.d.). Biological transistor enables computing within living cells, study says. Retrieved from https://med.stanford.edu/news/all-news/2013/03/biological-transistor-enables-computing-within-living-cells-study-says.html.
Panoutsos, K. (2016). *CRISPR germline alteration: Impact on human civilization*. San Francisco: Dolphin Publishing. Retrieved from: https://read.amazon.com/?asin=B01C3UPPIG.
Pasic, M. D., Samaan, S., & Yousef, G. M. (2013). Genomic Medicine: New Frontiers and New Challenges. *Clinical Chemistry*, 162–63. doi:10.1373/clinchem.2012.184622.
PCRN: Perkins Act. (n.d.). Retrieved from https://cte.ed.gov/legislation/about-perkins-iv.
Presentations & Webinars. 2017. (n.d.). Retrieved from http://www.ncperkins.org/course/view.php?id=31.
Ross, A. (2016). *The industries of the future*. New York: Simon & Schuster.
Venter, J. C. (2014). *Life at the speed of light: From the double helix to the dawn of digital life*. London: Abacus.
What Is Genomic Medicine? (n.d.). Retrieved from https://www.genome.gov/27552451/what-is-genomic-medicine/.

Chapter Six

Agricultural Genome

Ghada Gouda and Angelo Markantonakis

Food and agriculture production and sustainability are crucial to the future of society. Genome editing has many new articles in publication on the subject, as the benefits and risks of genome editing and food security are discussed.

The breaking of chromosomes, food intake, and production have an impact on the sustaining of the future as the population of the world continues to increase. "Genome editing provides new approaches to reach objectives in food security, but uncertainty among regulators and segments of the public regarding the associated benefits and risks may impede implementation" (Bogdanove, 2016, p. 1). Academic institutions will be at the forefront of agricultural genome scientific research.

Agricultural genome and editing within a linear progression of higher education, and short-term, mid-term, and long-term changes that are on the horizon, are all discussed. Over time, academic institutions have developed curriculum programs within the field to mimic ideals of agricultural genome and editing.

OVERVIEW OF CONTENT

An in-depth review of the agricultural and biotechnology curricula within the state of North Carolina is provided. How these changes will affect community colleges and senior institutions is highlighted. Advice for administrators within academic institutions, as well as for future students, is given. Interviews and campus visits with academic institutions, senior level educators, and programs within the field of the human genome have been conducted and are discussed.

Over the next thirty years, the population will increase drastically. Food consumption will be a major component to an increased population. "By 2050, a global population of 9.8 billion will demand 70% more food than is consumed today. Feeding this expanded population nutritiously and sustainably will require substantial improvements to the global food system—one that provides livelihoods for farmers as well as nutritious products for consumers" (Shaping the Future of Food Security and Agriculture, n.d.).

There is a wide range of methods that are utilized that impact the concept of agricultural genome. One of the methods is agricultural biotechnology. It is defined as "a range of tools, including traditional breeding techniques that alter living organisms, or parts of organisms, to make or modify products; improve plants or animals; or develop microorganisms for specific agricultural uses. Modern biotechnology today includes the tools of genetic engineering" (Agricultural Biotechnology Glossary, n.d.).

With an increase in the global population, agricultural biotechnology will be crucial in creating a sustainable food supply for the future. Molecular breeding will also impact the pace in which food will be processed.

Genomic selection (GS) operates on the principle that a large number of markers can be utilized to estimate breeding values (Bhat et al., 2016). Expediting the process and allowing for no need of prior understanding of where specific genes are located (Meuwissen et al., 2001). "The use of genome-wide DNA markers to predict genomic estimated breeding values (GEBV), first proposed by Meuwissen [Meuwissen et al., 2001] has radically changed perspectives in molecular breeding" (Bartholomé et al., 2016, p. 1).

The world faces an increased demand of food with limited land that is suitable for growing crops. Advances in marker technology and breeding methodology will remarkably increase crop production. Scientists have been working on improving genomic selection technologies, as it is believed that it may significantly increase the speed and process of creating plant and animal populations. In the process, predicting selection accuracy for crops and breeding through genetic dominance.

The Council of Agriculture Science and Technology (CAST) is working on improving genome editing in agriculture. CAST is a task force composed of sixty members. The CAST mission statement states: "CAST, through its network of experts, assembles, interprets, and communicates credible, balanced, science-based information to policymakers, the media, the private sector, and the public" (LLC—Ames, n.d.).

CAST has impacted U.S. legislation and federal agencies. CAST also provides many resources for agricultural productivity, and it is influential in many other initiatives relative to innovative technologies within agriculture. With so much involvement, and with the advances within agricultural genome practices, there will be many changes.

Higher education institutions will be a cornerstone in agricultural genome science as these changes occur. In the process, preparing an employable workforce within the future with new technologies in mind is imperative.

AGRICULTURAL GENOME IN HIGHER EDUCATION

Many initiatives look for ways to provide food sustainability by 2050. The need for an employable workforce that has the skills needed to use the innovative technology in agriculture necessitates changes in the higher education. Those changes will include adding, removing, and modifying academic programs. An in-depth review of the breadth of agricultural programs can be seen in the state of North Carolina.

Agricultural education has a foundation within Career and Technical Education (CTE) by introducing the concept from grades 7 through 12. Agricultural Education is designed to provide students with appropriate, comprehensive preparation for career and postsecondary education in the agriculture, food, and natural resources careers cluster. All Agricultural Education courses are contained in the following five career pathways:

- Agribusiness Systems
- Animal Systems
- Natural Resources Systems
- Plant Systems
- Power, Structural, and Technical Systems (Agricultural Education, n.d.).

The curricula mentioned above, as well as organizations such as the Future Farmers of America (FFA), attempt to introduce students to available opportunities within agriculture. The FFA provides agricultural education and alignments for students to grow and gain exposure to careers in agricultural education.

In reviewing the North Carolina Community College System (NCCCS) education catalog, two coded areas—Agricultural and Natural Resources Technology #15 and Biological and Chemical Technologies #20—are combined, and both coded areas contain twenty-nine programs relative to areas within agriculture. Some specific programs are:

- Agribusiness Technology (A15100)
- Agriculture Education (A15410)
- Sustainable Agriculture (A15240)
- Horticulture Technology (A15240)
- Agricultural Biotechnology (A20110)
- Biotechnology (A20100)

- Environmental Management Technology (A20230) (Sayers, 2018).

Even though the NCCCS has twenty-nine dedicated curricula within the fields of agriculture and biotechnology, the future of agriculture is unstable: "North Carolina appears to be at a literal crossroads regarding its agricultural future. Although North Carolina is a national agricultural leader, and the state is highly dependent on agricultural output for jobs and revenue" (Gergen et al., 2017, p. 1). With the incorporation of CTE certificates and Work-Based Learning (WBL) opportunities, there is hope to rectify the needs of North Carolina through agriculture.

Technology Initiatives

Technology advancement and innovation necessitate considering programs and curriculum changes in higher education. Initiatives also are being created as catalysts for change as businesses and processes align.

> Today's agriculture routinely uses sophisticated technologies such as robots, temperature and moisture sensors, aerial images, and GPS technology. These advanced devices and precision agriculture and robotic systems allow businesses to be more profitable, efficient, safer, and more environmentally friendly. (National Institute of Food and Agriculture, n.d.)

Agricultural developments need to adapt to the changes in technology in order to compete with innovation, sustainable food resources, and environmental concerns.

Functional genomic initiatives are currently funded to influence the opportunities such as curing genetic diseases, improving agricultural production, and providing life sciences research. Washington State University has invested $30 million of internal funding in promising research and student initiatives within competitive research opportunities.

> The initiative will develop critical core infrastructure for the application of this cutting edge gene-editing technology to support all life sciences research at WSU. It will also enable the university to build a cohort of faculty to drive basic and applied research and to communicate and address social and ethical approaches regarding gene-enhanced food animals. (Next Generation Variety Development and Education for Grains, Apples, Alternative Crops, and Cool Season Legumes)

It is proactive initiatives such as Washington State's peer-reviewed proposal competition that will spearhead educational research opportunities for students. In addition, it will assist the university in recruiting faculty.

Short Term (1–5 Years)

The Plant and Animal Genomes (PAG) meeting in its twenty-sixth year was the ag-genomics' largest meeting: "With 167 different scientific workshops over 6 days covering all major agriculturally important species . . . from the record-breaking attendance at PAG XXVI of more than 3,100 scientists to the breadth of the research highlighted, we predict that agricultural genomics will continue to accelerate" (Beiki et al., 2018).

The PAG meeting illustrates how strong the research is, as well as the impact currently occurring within agricultural genome studies. The PAG workshops allow a healthy platform for networking opportunities, collegiality, and scientific inquiry among peers.

According to Eurofins Genomics, an international provider of genomics services, the following topic areas are a compilation of research and technology innovations relative to the agricultural genome:

- Genomic, transcriptomic, and metagenomic characterization of plant, pathogens, and microorganisms with next-generation sequencing or array technologies
- Trait marker identification and genotyping (SNPs, SSRs, InDels, etc.)
- Genomic selection/genomics-based breeding/genome-wide association markers
- DNA extraction from leaves, seeds, soil, insects, and all other materials
- Bioinformatics
- Sanger and gene-sequencing solutions
- Genetic inserts identification and characterization
- Seed quality and purity testing
- GMO genetic characterization and testing
- PCR assay (including quantitative and real-time PCR) development, validation, and conduction
- DNA and RNA oligonucleotides, gene synthesis, and vector construction (DNA & RNA Oligonucleotides—Quality You Can Trust, n.d.).

Eurofins assists as genomics support to the crop industry and plant-based research. Having identified so many areas of services needed illustrates how quickly change in a short-term period can occur. There will be a need for higher education institutions to make decisions quickly to serve student populations that will seek training and employability skills within agriculture-related avenues.

Plants that have a longer shelf life is one example of innovative technology within genetic engineering: "In perspective, lots of fruits and food items are on our table because genetic engineering helped it survive the onslaught of virus or helped to preserve its life" (Panoutsos, 2016, p. 193). Though this is a short-term change, it has a long-term potential impact on the future of agricultural genomics. Current research indicates that food sustainability will be the next wave of changes relative to food supply and consumption.

Mid-Term (5–10 Years)

North Carolina State University (NCSU)—The NCSU Plants for Human Health Institute (PHHI) is part of an integrated effort to utilize emerging technologies for plant improvement and human health benefits. Currently, Dr. Debora Esposito, assistant professor at NCSU, has a lab within PHHI sequencing the blueberry genome.

> The role of the institute is to develop a new generation of fruits and vegetables that are pharmacologically active in dietary levels of intake, and to investigate medical plant resources from sources around the globe which may have a place in the future American marketplace. Researchers use advanced scientific tools to gain new insight into cellular processes, and then translate these breakthroughs through genomics and plant breeding into plants with desired traits. (Writer, n.d.)

Dr. Esposito's current research is analyzing commercial blueberries versus Alaskan blueberries. "These projects are Bill and Melinda Gates Foundation funded. We are trying to find the good chemicals of foods to enhance their consumption" (D. Esposito, personal communication, July 2, 2018). This research will allow for the food-consumption industries to see the benefits of organic sources.

As stated above with regard to short-term changes, enhanced consumption properties will be a focal point for researchers within the near future. The current research conducted at PHHI examines the impact of blueberry and green tea polyphenols, which are a "class of naturally occurring chemicals in plants that provide health benefits when eaten" (The North Carolina Research Campus, n.d.). The research has received grants from NASA and the U.S. Army.

The ideals behind foods with the possibilities of a longer shelf life has NASA asking for outcomes: "Recently NASA has asked for us to review the types of foods astronauts are eating. To enhance the quality and nutrients of their foods" (D. Esposito, personal communication, July 2, 2018). NCSU and PHHI stress the need to build partnerships for resources and for further research of this kind.

Dr. Esposito discusses the research conducted at PHHI within the local community: "We do a lot locally in the community with sweet potato and watermelons, trying to do the same process" (D. Esposito, personal communication, July 2, 2018). Research on nutrient levels, shelf life, and the quality of food is gaining traction.

The phenomena of 3D food printing, along with other innovative processes such as the research by Dr. Esposito mentioned above, may serve as agricultural genomic approaches that are possible solutions for food needs in the future. These approaches are potentially answering the questions on whether or not sustainable food sources are possible.

Long Term (10–20 Years)

Technologies such as transcription activator-like effector nucleases (TALENs), and Zinc-Finger Nucleases (ZFN), are examples of genome editing methods: "ZFNs, and TALENs were instrumental in establishing successful approaches to plant and animal genome editing" (Bogdanove, 2018, p. 3).

In addition, the clustered regularly interspaced short palindromic repeat (CRISPR) and the associated protein 9 (Cas9) system together are used as an effective genome editing tool in agriculture genomes: "Among the three existing types of CRISPR/Cas9 systems, the type II system involving Cas9 proteins has proven to be the most promising genome engineering tool" (Kruminis-Kaszkiel et al., 2018, p. 2). Modifying genomes illustrates the lengths at which long-term change is always imminent.

The importance of genome modification could be life-altering for the world.

> Gene modification can make the magic needed to change the crops into tough drought resistant varieties that give big yield. Scientists were able to raise the sugar accumulation within tubers by altering just one gene. They went on to stop cancer producing agents through subsequent alterations. These techniques make the crops more pest resistant and nutrient rich. (Panoutsos, 2016, p. 701)

TALENs and ZFN will be at the forefront of agricultural genomic-editing processes. Editing will continue to evolve with time. So will the improvements to the technologies and tools utilized within the research being conducted.

AGRICULTURAL GENOMICS IN HEALTH CARE

The health-care industry is working toward a nutritional core of assisting individuals with their long-term health preventive practices. "The main idea is to find out what type of diet suggestions for nutrition are available. Food consumption issues are the reason for malnourished food choices" (D. Esposito, personal communication, July 2, 2018). Genetically Modified Organisms (GMOs) and processed foods are other main factors to the need for a nutritional core.

"Shifting to nutritionally and genetically based health care can prevent disease and promote healthy living" (The North Carolina Research Campus, n.d.).

Instruction on cooking, meal preparation, and an understanding of the good chemicals in foods is needed. In advancing technology, the health-care industry will benefit from improved agricultural genomes in many fields such as food safety, healthy-balanced food, disease prevention, and treatment.

Diet and food nutrition science concepts mesh well with the World Economic Forum's initiative of efficient and nutritious foods.

> The World Economic Forum's System Initiative on Shaping the Future of Food is to build inclusive, sustainable, efficient and nutritious food systems through leadership-driven, market-based action and collaboration, informed by insights and innovation, in alignment with the Sustainable Development Goals. (Shaping the Future of Food Security and Agriculture, n.d.)

The combination of nutrigenomics and preventative practices will create lasting changes in the methods that health-care practitioners incorporate into their diagnostic routines and treatment plans.

AGRICULTURAL GENOMICS IN HUMAN PHARMACEUTICALS

The use of plant molecular farming to produce therapeutic proteins is improving. The production of plant medication has greatly increased. Research on food and plants in drug improvement is growing in fields such as vaccines, disease treatment, and prevention. "The concept of using plants to produce recombinant pharmaceutical proteins, referred to as plant molecular farming (PMF) or pharming (PMP), is not new. Human growth hormon [was] initially produced in tobacco and sunflower in 1986" (Yao et al., 2015, p. 28550).

Herbal medicine uses natural products instead of chemical or synthetically modified options for treatment. The importance of identifying specific plants within medicine allows for expedited information on possible treatments, preventions, and cures.

> Extensive research on DNA-based molecular markers is in progress in many research institutes all over the world. DNA-based molecular markers have a great utility in the herbal drug analysis and widely used for the authentication of plant species of medicinal importance. (Srivastava & Mishra, 2009, p. 1)

Deoxyribonucleic acid (DNA) markers can assist in highlighting genetic traits that can be identified for future scientific research. Plant selection could become quicker, improving the research on plants and possible pharmaceutical research.

GREEN ENERGY

The term *green energy* could have a whole new meaning ten years from now. The idea of trees or modified plants lighting walkways is not far away. However, there are concerns over the genetic modifications and implications in the future for reproducing these types of plants. The ability to mass-produce plants of this nature on a large scale is challenging.

BARRIERS AND CHALLENGES OF AGRICULTURAL GENOME

Genome editing and genetic engineering have a promising future in improving agriculture and plants sciences. There are some specific challenges and barriers, as discussed below, that may impact their use.

Climate Change

Crop yields, farming production, and consumer forecasting are all impacted by the weather. Drastic changes can destroy the output of farms and the amount of available food. Coupled with these possibilities are the effects of climate change. It is predicted that the global temperature is most likely going to increase over the next couple of decades. Food security and plants may be impacted with the increased temperature reducing the production of many crops.

Limited Water

The future of water resources predicts a significant shortage of water that may affect two-thirds of the world's population. Immediate and critical actions must be taken to find ways to manage water and other water resources.

Food and Nutritional Issues

Wasted food leads to hunger and a negative economic impact. In addition, "reducing the world's 1.3 billion tons of wasted food every year may hold the key to sustainably feeding 9 billion people by 2050, according to new interviews from the Institute of Food Technologists (IFT)–sponsored FutureFood 2050 initiative" (Food Waste, 2014).

The FutureFood 2050 Initiative, along with other initiatives, aims to assist in securing the sustainability of food resources and reducing nutritional issues such as underweight or overweight populations or malnutrition that may be a result of a lack of healthy food accessibility and sustainability. The future of humanity necessitates establishing strategies on reducing waste, increasing awareness, and finding alternative resources.

CHANGES AFFECTING THE COMMUNITY COLLEGE AND THE UNIVERSITY

Curriculum programs within an academic institution will feel the ripple of changes within the agricultural genome science. Areas such as credentialing and employment opportunities will impact community colleges in their development of viable academic programs for enrollment. Technology, internships, and barriers to these programs must be acknowledged for community colleges to prepare for short-, mid-, and long-term change.

Credentialing

The fields of biotechnology and agricultural as stated above within the state of North Carolina have twenty-nine relatable programs available for students. There is not a recognized industry standard for credentials. The lack of a standardized credential for students leaves the potential positions for community college students in a state of uncertainty. This is best described by Dr. Carol Scherczinger, the dean of arts and sciences at Rowan-Cabarrus Community College.

> One of the biggest challenges in any biotech field is the lack of industry-recognized certifications or standards, which would credential community college students. Most of these positions start at the bachelor's level. Academia and industry would need to buy in to the concept that community colleges can do a very good job training bench-level technicians. (C. Scherczinger, personal communication, July 2, 2018)

Community colleges will need to work together with local industries within biotechnology and agriculture to create industry standards that will allow students opportunities for employment.

EMPLOYMENT OPPORTUNITIES FOR STUDENTS

Agriculture and agribusiness are strong areas of employment. It would be wise for community colleges to build partnerships with career profile organizations to highlight and showcase curriculum programs. There are also more employment opportunities than graduates. "Nearly 60,000 High-Skilled Agriculture Job Openings Expected Annually in U.S., yet only 35,000 Graduates Available to fill them" (USDA 2015–2020 Employment Opportunities—in Food, Agriculture, Renewable Natural Resources, and the Environment, n.d.).

It would be beneficial to students if they could review career profiles relative to the curriculum programs, degrees, and credentials that prospective students are interested in obtaining.

> According to a study by North Carolina State University, agriculture and agribusiness provides 663,000 jobs—17 percent of all jobs in the state. This is topped only by education and healthcare with 765,000 jobs (though North Carolina is also a top agricultural educator, which contributes to the growth of this industry). (Gergen et al., 2017)

Community colleges must also work to incorporate innovative technologies and training into the programs being offered at academic institutions as mentioned within short-term change in the agricultural genome.

Internships

Internship opportunities allow for students to apply the knowledge gained within the classroom setting to real-world applications. Considering the lab-intensive setting with agricultural genomics and technological innovations, students will need exposure to a wide variety of experiences. Strong partnerships with local businesses and employers will create a gateway for student employability.

> We have strong partnerships with Rowan Cabarrus Community College. We take the student with the skills and experiences they gain in their associate degree for laboratory partnerships. The internship is the first door. We have at least three lab technicians from RCCC. All three have got job offers. It is a great way to start. (D. Esposito, personal communication, July 2, 2018)

The knowledge that students gain from an internship allows for them to gain experiences, expertise, and network toward future employment within their fields of interest. The more knowledgeable a student becomes, the more they become marketable within their field of study.

ADVICE TO ADMINISTRATORS OF COMMUNITY COLLEGES AND UNIVERSITIES

As stated above, employment will be a growing concern as students try to make career choices and future decisions about their job prospects as they take their roles within the community. "The demands of leadership have changed . . . what will matter about these issues will be how they affect job growth more than how they affect family, political, and religious values" (Clifton, 2011, p. 3).

Considering that technology, and many of the challenges discussed above that will be present for academic administrators, the reality may be that curriculum programs may not be needed within the field of agricultural genome. From an administrative perspective, Dr. Michael Quillen, the vice president of academic affairs at Rowan-Cabarrus Community College, describes it this way:

> Don't be attracted by shiny things. It is important that a Community College provides good programs with well-evaluated learning and employment outcomes—and that there is a match to the jobs and needs of the community. Make sure the jobs are there for graduates, and that the programs created are of the best quality. (M. Quillen, personal communication, July 17, 2018)

As mentioned above, employment opportunities and prospective internships for students look promising. Dr. Quillen's message suggests that administrators need to make well-informed, fiscally responsible decisions on academic program investments.

Technology and Opportunities

The automation of jobs will impact employment opportunities. Innovation and an increase in the use of robotics will be a piece of the employment landscape for students. Dr. Carol Scherczinger discussed how automation may impact database processing.

> There are very strict education and training requirements for an analyst (anyone who evaluates and reports results). However, with state database laws expanding, there is a great need for front-end processing of large numbers of samples. Automation is becoming an increasing reality. (C. Scherczinger, personal communication, July 2, 2018)

Advances in technology will impact agricultural production, food sustainability, and potential student employment opportunities.

Support Programs

Administrators within academic institutions will want to review resources and how to work with businesses, companies, and the needs of the community. Academically and from an agricultural perspective, administrators will need to be aware of the messages they communicate and their actions.

> Instruct courses on how to cook and use things. Discuss waste, and price costs. Walk the talk. Right now there are vending machines that are full of junk. There are more than 100 people here without a place to get a meal. Be available. Listen. Have more accountability to the community. Integrate environ-

mental. The same way we provide good internet and resources. There is a need to provide good foods. Think of the community format. Creat possible gardens. (D. Esposito, personal communication, July 2, 2018)

Administration must align the communications and actions of their academic institutions in ways that illustrate accountability toward a united stance of support for all of the programs that are offered. It will be crucial for administrators to review the viability of the curriculum programs that their academic institutions offer.

There will need to be a watchful eye on technology, automation, and how both pieces will impact future employment opportunities of enrolled degree-seeking students. Lastly, administrators will want to make sure their messages of support are clear regarding all of the programs offered and the actions of the campus culture as a whole.

ADVICE TO STUDENTS IN COMMUNITY COLLEGES AND UNIVERSITIES

An interview conducted by NCSU's College of Agricultural and Life Sciences (CALS) with Rachel Grantham, an agronomist for Smithfield Hog Production Division's Smithfield Agronomics program, highlights six specific components that she advises students to take into consideration if they choose to pursue interests within agriculture. They are:

1. Your classes, grades, and extracurricular activities are important.
2. The profession you dream of as an incoming freshman doesn't have to be the one you choose upon graduation.
3. Take a job or internship in something different from your main interest.
4. Participate.
5. Find a mentor.
6. Dress sharp, proceed with confidence, and make those connections. (Kellner, 2017)

The six components proposed here are also noticeable within the NCCCS WBL course formats listed above in discussing agricultural genome in higher education. Students must seek internships and opportunities to gain exposure to agriculture career opportunities.

A Global Concern Needs a Global Student

Students must learn about international as well as national advancements in agriculture and plant genome sciences. Students need to learn what other nations are doing regarding agriculture sciences and food production and how they use genetic editing in agriculture. What students learn will enlighten their minds to new ideas and technologies.

> The word is innovation. The way we eat has completely changed. We need to understand the need for feeding. With all the GMOs and processed food. There is still malnutrition. Get educated. Teach others how to eat. . . . Use the cell phone to teach about food. The innovation for delivering foods and the processes . . . (D. Esposito, personal communication, July 2, 2018)

Moving forward, agriculture genome editing, and agriculture research jobs may introduce new promising jobs to the future generations. It is now a competition not only between businesses and nations, but also a competition between the whole world and the future challenges that we may face globally. Technological innovation and the use of cell phones may be the bridge that students will need to meld their education, employment options, and future decisions.

CONCLUSION

Barriers and challenges of agricultural genome will be global issues as the population increases. Sustainable food sources, technological advances, genome research, the supply of water, and employment are all areas that will be affected by agricultural changes.

> If the population grows as expected to more than 9 billion people over the next 30 years, the amount of food produced will need to increase by 70 percent lest the world grow even hungrier. This comes in the midst of climate change, as temperatures rise and potable water becomes an ever scarcer resource (70 percent of freshwater used globally goes toward agriculture). (Ross, 2017, p. 161)

The short-, mid-, and long-term changes that will take place within agriculture will influence many areas within higher education. As mentioned above, credentialing, employment opportunities, and internships will have the most noticeable influences regarding agriculture programs.

Higher education administration must align the needs of the academic institution with the program offerings that are viable and in the best interest of the students and community. Students must be open-minded on the opportunities available within agriculture. Students may benefit from internships and utilizing their technology such as cell phones to learn and become educated about healthy choices for food.

CHAPTER SUMMARY

- With an increase in the global population, agricultural biotechnology will be crucial in creating a sustainable food supply for the future.
- The world faces an increased demand of food with limited land that is suitable for growing crops.
- The Council of Agriculture Science and Technology (CAST) is working on improving genome editing in agriculture.
- Higher education institutions will be a cornerstone in the agricultural genome science as the changes occur.
- Agricultural developments need to adapt to the changes in technology in order to compete with innovation, sustainable food resources, and environmental concerns.
- Eurofins assist in providing genomics support to the crop industry in plant-based research.
- Plants with a longer shelf life is an example of innovative technologies within genetic engineering.
- The ideals behind foods with the possibilities of a longer shelf life has NASA asking for outcomes.
- The phenomenon of 3D food printing along with other innovative processes may prove useful in agricultural genomic approaches that are possible solutions for food needs in the future.
- The health-care industry is working toward a nutritional core of assisting individuals with long-term health preventive practices.
- The combination of nutrigenomics and preventive practices will create lasting changes in the methods that health-care practitioners incorporate into their diagnostic routines and treatment plans.
- Herbal medicine uses natural products instead of chemical or synthetically modified options for treatment.
- The importance of identifying specific plants within medicine allows for expedited information and possible treatments, preventions, and cures.
- The idea of trees or modified plants lighting walkways is not far in the future.
- The future of water resources predicts a significant shortage of water that may affect two-thirds of the world's population.
- Wasted food leads to hunger and a negative economic impact.
- The future of humanity necessitates establishing strategies and reducing waste, increasing awareness, and finding alternative resources.
- Curriculum programs within higher education will feel the ripple effect of changes within the agricultural genome science.
- Community colleges will need to work together with local industries within the biotechnology area to create industry standards that will allow students to obtain opportunities for employment.

- Internship opportunities allow for students to apply the knowledge gained within the classroom setting to real-world application.
- The knowledge that students gain from an internship allows them to gain experiences and expertise, and then network toward future employment within their fields of interest.
- The automation of jobs will impact employment opportunities.
- Administrators within higher education will want to review resources and how to work with businesses, companies, and the needs of the community.
- There will need to be a watchful eye on technology, automation, and how both pieces impact the future employment opportunities of enrolled degree-seeking students.
- Students must learn about international as well as national advancements in agriculture and plant genome sciences.
- Moving forward, agricultural genome editing in agricultural research jobs may introduce new promising opportunities to future generations.
- Administrators in higher education must align the needs of the academic institution with program offerings that are viable, and in the best interest of the students and the community.

REFERENCES

Agricultural Biotechnology Glossary. (n.d.). Retrieved from https://www.usda.gov/topics/biotechnology/biotechnology-glossary.

Agricultural Education. (n.d.). Retrieved from http://www.dpi.state.nc.us/cte/program-areas/agricultural/.

Bartholomé, J., Heerwaarden, J. V., Isik, F., Boury, C., Vidal, M., Plomion, C., & Bouffier, L. (2016). Performance of genomic prediction within and across generations in maritime pine. *BMC Genomics, 17*(1). doi:10.1186/s12864-016-2879-8.

Beiki, H., Eveland, A. L., & Tuggle, C. K. (2018, April 10). Recent advances in plant and animal genomics are taking agriculture to new heights. Retrieved from https://genomebiology.biomedcentral.com/articles/10.1186/s13059-018-1427-z.

Bhat, J. A., Ali, S., Salgotra, R. K., Mir, Z. A., Dutta, S., Jadon, V., . . . Prabhu, K. V. (2016). Genomic Selection in the Era of Next Generation Sequencing for Complex Traits in Plant Breeding. *Frontiers in Genetics, 7*. doi:10.3389/fgene.2016.00221.

Bogdanove, A. (2016, April). *CAST The Science Source for Food, Agriculture, and Environmental Issues* (PDF). Retrieved from https://www.cast-science.org/media//cms/CAST_AI_Genome_Editing_Funding_Pros_F3C6DBE342104.pdf.

Bogdanove, A. (2018, July). *Genome Editing in Agriculture: Methods, Applications, and Governance* (Working paper No. 60). Retrieved http://www.cast-science.org/file.cfm/media/products/digitalproducts/CAST_IP60_Gene_Editing_D752224D52A53.pdf.

Clifton, J. (2011). *Coming Jobs War*. New York: Gallup Press.

DNA & RNA Oligonucleotides—Quality You Can Trust. (n.d.). Retrieved from https://www.eurofinsgenomics.eu/en/dna-rna-oligonucleotides/.

Food Waste. (2014, September 10). Retrieved from https://futurefood2050.com/interviews/food-waste/.

Gergen, C., & Correspondents, S. M. (2017, March 26). If NC wants to feed itself—and the world—it needs to save its farms. Retrieved from https://www.newsobserver.com/news/business/article140522363.html.

Kellner, C. (2017, March 06). College of Agriculture and Life Sciences News. Retrieved from https://cals.ncsu.edu/news/agpack-strong-rachel-granthams-advice-to-students/.
Kruminis-Kaszkiel, E., Juranek, J., Maksymowicz, W., & Wojtkiewicz, J. (2018, March). CRISPR/Cas9 Technology as an Emerging Tool for Targeting Amyotrophic Lateral Sclerosis. Retrieved from https://www.ncbi.nlm.nih.gov/pmc/articles/PMC5877767/.
LLC—Ames. (n.d.). CAST. Retrieved from http://www.cast-science.org/about/.
Meuwissen, T. H., Hayes, B. J., & Goddard, M. E. (2001, April 01). Prediction of Total Genetic Value Using Genome-Wide Dense Marker Maps. Retrieved from http://www.genetics.org/content/157/4/1819.
National Institute of Food and Agriculture. (n.d.). Retrieved from https://nifa.usda.gov/topic/agriculture-technology.
Next Generation Variety Development and Education for Grains, Apples, Alternative Crops, and Cool Season Legumes—Washington State University. (2016, February 15). Retrieved from https://reeis.usda.gov/web/crisprojectpages/1008828-next-generation-variety-development-and-education-for-grains-apples-alternative-crops-and-cool-season-legumes.html.
Panoutsos, K. (2016). *CRISPR germaline alteration: Impact on human civilization.* San Francisco: Dolphin Publishing. Retrieved from: https://read.amazon.com/?asin=B01C3UPPIG.
Ross, A. (2017). *The industries of the future.* New York: Simon & Schuster.
Sayers, R. (2018, July 16). NC Community College System Catalog. Retrieved from https://www.nccommunitycolleges.edu/academic-programs/nc-community-college-system-catalog.
Shaping the Future of Food Security and Agriculture. (n.d.). Retrieved from https://www.weforum.org/system-initiatives/shaping-the-future-of-food-security-and-agriculture.
Srivastava, S., & Mishra, N. (2009). *Genetic Markers—A Cutting-Edge Technology in Herbal Drug Research.* Retrieved from http://www.jocpr.com/articles/genetic-markers--a-cuttingedge-technology-in-herbal-drug-research.pdf.
The North Carolina Research Campus. (n.d.). Retrieved from http://www.NCResearchCampus.net/.
USDA 2015–2020 Employment Opportunities—in Food, Agriculture, Renewable Natural Resources, and the Environment. (n.d.). Retrieved from https://www.purdue.edu/usda/employment/.
Writer, S. (n.d.). Home. Retrieved from http://plantsforhumanhealth.ncsu.edu/.
Yao, J., Weng, Y., Dickey, A., & Wang, K. Y. (2015, December 02). Plants as Factories for Human Pharmaceuticals: Applications and Challenges. Retrieved from http://www.mdpi.com/1422-0067/16/12/26122/htm.

Chapter Seven

Bitcoin/Blockchain

Darrel W. Staat

In 2008, an unknown person or group, using the alias of Satoshi Nakamoto, created a method of cryptocurrency that has since become known as Bitcoin/blockchain. It was a computerized method of transferring money from one person or source to another without the use of cash, checks, money orders, or any other form of moving funds from one location to another. No bank, financial organization, or third party was included in the transaction. The process was protected by cryptography and groupings of transactions placed in blocks, which were electronically connected to each other and could not be changed once made (Tapscott & Tapscott, 2016).

Once in place, the value of Bitcoin increased significantly until it stood at almost $300 billion in late 2017; however, during 2018, it freefell to $112 billion in October (Kharif & Leising, 2018). A Bitcoin, which in December 2017 was worth almost $20,000, dropped to $3,400 in late 2018, an 80 percent decrease. The fear was that it was going to drop even more in 2019 to perhaps $1,500 (CNN Business, 2018). The new funding method was suddenly in trouble due to issues of internal operation and external mistrust. Some critics called the entire process a fraud from the start (Kharif & Leising, 2018).

There is little doubt that Bitcoin/blockchain still faces rough sledding in 2019. However, out of the experience of this early attempt at cryptocurrency comes a silver lining. If Bitcoin is headed for disaster, the blockchain process used for holding and transferring funds is being heralded as a greatly improved way of storing and exchanging digital information, including birth certificates, high school and higher education diplomas, portfolios of experience, health records, publications, and anything else that can be digitized that is important to an individual. Blockchain has the potential to become the premiere secure location to hold and share all things digital.

According to Alexandra Perry (2018), for those ready to try blockchain, here are the facts:

1. Blockchain is a powerful technology that allows information to be stored safely and securely.
2. Because of blockchain's structure, the information stored on a blockchain can remain public.
3. Because many blockchain technologies are decentralized, users can connect and exchange information without a central government (Perry, 2018, p. 4).

Think of blockchain as a type of distributed ledger that, rather than being held in a centralized organization such as a bank or a hospital, is now a decentralized database held in a network of computers that can be accessed by its owner. Blockchain can be used for the distribution of money, but it can also store and distribute any type of digitalized data.

> With blockchain an organization will not be confirming transactions or data. The public verifies and time stamps transactions. The public essentially is thousands of globally dispersed computers or nodes, which are mostly anonymous. Once the data is validated by participating nodes in the network, the transaction is added to a block. The new block is then permanently added to the blockchain and distributed to the entire network. The added block is chained to the previous block via cryptography, hence the name block chain. (Moy, 2018, p. 1)

The big question is, what will happen to Bitcoin? Its fate will be determined in the next decade. Either this cryptocurrency will find a way through the various issues it faces, or it will develop into just a limited method of storing and distributing money that does not scale. If that happens, Bitcoin will have value only to a small set of users. Time will tell whether Bitcoin becomes a major player in the storing and distribution of money or not. Its competition may develop its way into success. By 2030, Bitcoin may be remembered as an initial attempt at cryptocurrency that failed, or perhaps the leader in the cryptocurrency world.

BLOCKCHAIN AND HIGHER EDUCATION

Although the question of Bitcoin will take some time to resolve, the concept of blockchain will most likely develop rapidly, as it is useful in many other areas than just the storing and distribution of money. It can be used to store and disseminate digital information for personal, governmental, business, and health reasons, as well as a variety of other possibilities. Higher education has taken notice, as well. Some faculty and students are extremely interested in the topic.

According to Search for Degrees Now:

> Blockchain is the paradigm-disrupting technology that is on everyone's mind, dominating the headlines in tech publications, and making investors get that tingly feeling. But, if you're an accounting student wondering where and how you can add blockchain expertise to your resume, you may feel a bit out to sea. Where are the university blockchain courses? (Search for Degrees Now, 2018, p. 2)

Blockchain has the potential to make current accounting programs obsolete. A number of universities in the United States are now offering either courses or programs in blockchain. These include Cornell University, Duke University, Georgetown University, MIT, New York University, Princeton University, Stanford University, University of California at Berkeley, and University of Illinois at Urbana-Champaign (Search for Degrees Now, 2018). Even a community college has gotten into the blockchain arena: "Central New Mexico Community College delivered blockchain-based diplomas in December 2017" (Bowman, 2018, p. 2).

Blockchain technology can be used in a number of ways by a community college or university. According to Kevin Roebuck in a *Wall Street Journal* article, there are five ways blockchain can be used in higher education: student records and credentialing, partnership platform, copyright and digital rights protection, course curricula, and the innovation learning platform (Roebuck, 2018).

1. **Student Records and Credentialing**. Blockchain offers a model for the secure collection and sharing of your competency indicators, including academic records, but also badges, certificates, citations, letters of recommendation, and the like. Think of it as an immutable, updatable, and verifiable e-portfolio of your learning-oriented life experiences.
2. **Partnership Platform**. Blockchain's peer-to-peer transaction-based model fits perfectly into . . . consortium efforts. Blockchain-based "smart contracts"—distributed, encrypted digital transactions among more than two parties—might be employed to ensure speed and transparency.
3. **Copyright and Digital Rights Protection**. Blockchain's ability to manage, share, and protect digital content makes it ideal for helping researchers, faculty members, and other higher-ed principals create intellectual property, share it, and still control the way it is used.
4. **Course Curricula**. Classes that teach the requisite blockchain programming skills will no doubt be important, but the technology presents a unique educational challenge because it sits at the intersec-

tion of so many areas of business and technology. . . . Thus, blockchain education requires an interdisciplinary approach.
5. **The Innovation Learning Platform**. Entrepreneurship is the lens through which many students view their educational opportunities. And many students see blockchain as preparation for the next generation of startups (Roebuck, 2018, p. 3).

Although these five blockchain uses are excellent possibilities, the list has increased. Don Tapscott and Alex Tapscott (2017) discussed the following: new pedagogy, costs, and a meta-university. Alicia Miranda (2018) identified data management and financial aid. The list will most likely increase on a continuing basis as time goes by and as the power of blockchain technology is better understood.

JOB MARKET

As community colleges and universities begin to offer courses and programs in the blockchain field, what are the possibilities that there will be jobs when students graduate? Accounting graduates especially should receive training and education in blockchain technology, as they are most likely to run into the blockchain in the business world, if not immediately, then in the near future. A concept as impressive and useful as the blockchain technology is will develop in the business world rapidly.

According to one researcher:

> The number of blockchain job listings doubled from 2016 to 2017, reaching nearly 5,000 jobs by the end of last year (*Forbes*). According to Emsi, IBM alone posted nearly 1,000 blockchain jobs in 2017, along with other major firms like Deloitte, Accenture and SAP also hiring in droves. (Burks, 2018, p. 2)

The jobs are already appearing and the chances for rapid increase in the numbers posted should increase significantly in the near future. Blockchain is coming into its own as a process and will most likely soon make a serious impact in the accounting processes used in business, industry, health, banking, and education. Community colleges and universities would be wise to take heed of this rapidly developing technology, as it will soon be demanded not only by the business community, but also by students across the nation.

According to another researcher:

> The technology [blockchain] is already being used to securely process financial transactions without the need for banks. Major supermarkets such as Walmart are using blockchain to track items in their food supply chain, and healthcare providers are exploring how blockchain might give patients greater ownership of their medical records. Even universities are getting in on the action

and using blockchain to issue degrees that can be easily verified by employers. (McKensie, 2018, p. 3)

The potential for blockchain appears to be endless. It could replace many accounting practices currently in operation. Further, it could replace recording processes now being used by business, industry, health organizations, educational institutions, and the like. It removes the middleman and decentralizes the ownership of information. As transparency and security become the norm in America and other societies across the globe, blockchain technology could play a very critical role.

The University of Pittsburgh has employed its assistant professor of chemical and petroleum engineering, Dr. Chris Wilmer, as the co-founder and managing editor of a journal called *Ledger*, which publishes peer-reviewed research on the subject of blockchain. The journal was initiated in 2014 and is available for review on the website of the University of Pittsburgh. For those interested, the *Ledger* is a source for the ongoing development of blockchain technology (McKensie, 2018).

THE FUTURE OF BLOCKCHAIN

Trying to predict where the blockchain technology will be in the next ten to twelve years on one hand is anybody's guess. However, two researchers have made an honest effort at doing just that. Both left their jobs at Gartner, a research firm, to become researchers of blockchain technology. They have made five predictions about the future of blockchain technology by the year 2030:

- **Prediction #1: Government Crypto**

    By 2030 most governments around the world will create or adopt some form of virtual currency. Compared to the traditional fiat alternative, cryptocurrency is more efficient, provides reduced settlement times, and offers increased traceability.

- **Prediction #2: Trillion-Dollar Protocols**

    By 2030, there will be more trillion-dollar tokens than there will be trillion-dollar companies. It [blockchain] dramatically reduces the costs of transactions and information flows. Large firms exist, in part, because there is a huge schism between processes that occur inside the walls versus those that cross to the outside.

- **Prediction #3: Blockchain Identity for All**

> By 2030, a cross-border, blockchain-based, self-sovereign identity standard will emerge for individual as well as physical and virtual assets. According to various sources, 1.5 billion people in the developing world lack proof of identity. . . . Blockchain-based self-sovereign identity platforms will provide the disenfranchised population with tools to obtain and maintain legal documentation.

- **Prediction #4: World Trade on Blockchain**

  > By 2030, most of the world trade will be conducted leveraging blockchain technology.

- **Prediction #5: Blockchain Used for Good**

  > By 2030, significant improvements in the world's standard of living will be attributable to the development of blockchain technology. Blockchain technology has the potential to shrink the poverty gap. How? It can be done by increasing financial inclusiveness, reducing corruption, and enabling decentralized access to value-creating assets (Valdes and Mitselmakher, 2018, p. 2).

Making predictions is always a risky business, but the five predictions listed above appear to have good chances of being on target. The year 2030 will tell. There may be other uses of the blockchain technology that have not been thought of yet, but they will appear to be almost self-evident in a few years. Whatever the case, community colleges and universities will need to stay abreast of the development of blockchain and be prepared to jump in to provide training and education as the needs develop. This is a technology to be watched carefully and consistently, not one to ignore.

ADVICE TO HIGHER EDUCATION ADMINISTRATORS

It appears that blockchain technology is here to stay, with its potential to improve accounting procedures and many other processes. When it becomes more obvious that the technology improves efficiency and reduces costs, the business community will be attracted to it. When it becomes obvious that blockchain can make health records easier to maintain as well as give the people individual ownership of them, the medical field will begin to make use of it. Banking systems are already looking into the technology to simplify and better secure its processes. It is only a matter of time before this technology is integrated into American society.

Higher education administrators should be paying close attention to this technology, as on both the community college and university levels there will be opportunities for courses and programs having to do with the technology.

Administrators need to be well informed and ready to develop courses and programs that will benefit the student, the business community, and the educational institution involved. By 2025, blockchain instruction should become another offering at the community college and university. By 2030, the programs and courses could be mainstreamed, accredited, and part and parcel of the various institutions.

ADVICE TO STUDENTS

Since students in general are looking ahead as best they can to employment opportunities resulting from their community college and university educations, blockchain will be on their lists of interest to pursue. Gauging exactly when students will be interested and which businesses and health organizations will be requiring the skills in blockchain for positions in their institutions will most likely vary by location. The institutions of higher education serving urban areas will probably see student and business interest first, but since successful ideas quickly move to other locations, whether the students and institutions are urban or rural will not make much difference.

The best advice students can receive is to include computer training in their educational experience. The digital world is here, and it will only expand its influence and impact as time goes by. Blockchain training will undoubtedly be in demand at many levels in the job market. It would benefit each student, no matter the area of interest, to spend as much time and coursework as possible learning the basics and more in this soon-to-be-critical field.

CONCLUSION

It took until the 1980s for the computer to become a necessary part of students' learning. Computers appeared in almost any field of study within a matter of a decade. It took until the 1990s for the internet to become an integral part of students' education, whether formal or informal. Within less than a decade, the internet invaded students' lives personally and educationally. It took until the 2000s for social media to appear. In a very few years, this, too, became so involved in everyone's lives that it is now impossible for most individuals to think about living without it.

Perhaps just when everyone wonders what else could possibly come that would have such an impact on the daily lives of human beings, enter blockchain. It will take until the 2030s for it to be fully implemented, but as it does, human beings will again be impacted and have to adapt. Is there no end to the technological changes that will impact businesses, health-care organizations, industries, and ultimately individuals? This book should help answer that question. There is still more to come. It will be critical to adapt and adopt.

CHAPTER SUMMARY

- A person or group using the alias of Satoshi Nakamoto created Bitcoin/blockchain in 2008.
- Bitcoin's value dropped from $20,000 in December 2017 to $3,400 in October 2018.
- Blockchain, on the other hand, increased in value as an accounting process.
- Blockchain is a kind of distributed ledger in a digital form.
- Higher education has taken notice of the blockchain phenomenon.
- Many universities and one community college have begun offering blockchain courses or programs.
- There are five ways that blockchain can be used in higher education, according to Kevin Roebuck.
- Other researchers have added more to the list.
- The blockchain job market doubled from 2016 to 2017.
- Major supermarkets are using blockchain to track items in their food supply chain.
- The University of Pittsburgh has produced a *Ledger* that publishes research on blockchain.
- Two researchers have published five predictions about the future of blockchain.
- Higher education administrators should be paying close attention to the development of blockchain.
- Students should consider training and education on the blockchain technology no matter what field they are studying in their community college or university.
- The 2020s will see the full development of the blockchain technology in business, health-care organizations, and higher education institutions.

REFERENCES

Bowman, L. (July 31, 2018). How blockchain is reshaping education. Retrieved from https://btcmanager.com/how-blockchain-is-reshaping-education.
Burks, H. (June 14, 2018). Blockchain 101: Decrypting the buzz for higher education. Retrieved from https://convergeconsulting.org/2018/06/14/blockchain-higher-education/.
CNN Business. (December 7, 2018). Bitcoin's epic plunge continues. Retrieved from https://www.cnn.com/2018/12/07/investing/bitcoin-prices-plunging/index.html.
Kharif, O., & Leising, M. (November 2, 2018) Bitcoin and Blockchain. Retrieved from https://www.bloomberg.com/quicktake/bitcoins.
McKensie, L. (August 13, 2018). Blockchain gains currency in higher ed. Retrieved from https://www.insidehighered.com/news/2018/08/13/rising-profile-blockchain-academe.

Miranda, A. (October 9, 2018). What is the blockchain and how can it transform higher education? Retrieved from https://www.academicimpressions.com/blog/what-is-blockchain-and-how-can-it-transform-higher-education/.

Moy, J. (February 2, 2018). Forget bitcoin, it's all about the blockchain. Retrieved from https://www.forbes.com/sites/jamiemoy/2018/02/22/forget-bitcoin-its-all-about-the-blockchain/#5fe20aa95f6b.

Perry, A. (January 6, 2018). Beyond bitcoin: Blockchain 2018. Retrieved from https://www.wealthdaily.com/articles/beyond-bitcoin-blockchain-2018/90697.

Roebuck, K. (May 7, 2018). 5 ways blockchain is revolutionizing higher education. Retrieved from https://partners.wsj.com/oracle/5-ways-blockchain-revolutionizing-higher-education/.

Search for Degrees Now. (2018). 10+ Universities offering blockchain courses. Retrieved from https://www.accounting-degree.org/college-cryptocurrency-blockchain-courses/.

Tapscott, D., & Tapscott, A. (2016). *Blockchain revolution: How technology behind bitcoin is changing money, business and the world*. New York: Penguin Random House LLC.

Tapscott, D., & Tapscott, A. (2017). The blockchain revolution and higher education. Retrieved from https://er.educause.edu/articles/2017/3/the-blockchain-revolution-and-higher-education.

Valdes, R., & Mitselmakher, K. (April 6, 2018). The future of blockchain technology: Top five predictions for 2030. Retrieved from https://medium.com/the-future-of-blockchain-technology-top-five/the-future-of-blockchain-technology-top-five-predictions-for-2030-67df1d7c2391.

Chapter Eight

Artificial Intelligence

Kira Ferris and Dahmon King

Artificial Intelligence is a constellation of technologies—from machine learning to natural language processing—that allows machines to sense, comprehend, act, and learn. As these technologies become simpler and smarter, and interfaces become more usable to consumers, the customer experience will improve.

Using algorithms, Artificial Intelligence is like a smart sponge; the more data it absorbs, the more intelligent it becomes. Artificial Intelligence equips users with information and answers at an alarming speed, so the users may spend more time on activities that add value to the company or learning institution. Most machinery in the past could never compete with the abilities of Artificial Intelligence. These interactions will continue to improve as this technology becomes more embedded in our environment and daily activities.

This chapter explores Artificial Intelligence by providing an overview of the discipline, insight into the current situation, the future of Artificial Intelligence, the ethics of Artificial Intelligence, changes in Artificial Intelligence, effects of Artificial Intelligence on community colleges and senior institutions, and advice for administration, faculty, and students.

THE STATUS OF ARTIFICIAL INTELLIGENCE

Currently, Artificial Intelligence (AI) consists of very powerful computers that can accomplish specific tasks. For example, in 1997, the computer Deep Blue won a series of chess games against Garry Kasparov, the world's chess champion for many years (Kasparov, 2017). In 2011, an even more powerful computer, Watson, competed against two of the best players in the game *Jeopardy* and beat them both (Baker, 2011). Since then, the Watson computer has been reprogrammed with information pertaining to cancer, and it now assists oncologists with data that helps them improve decisions on appropriate procedures for working with cancer patients.

Both Deep Blue and Watson are examples of narrow AI. That is, they are extremely powerful, but they can only accomplish very specific tasks such as winning at chess, coming out on top in a game show like *Jeopardy*, or providing extensive background information to a medical doctor. There are many other examples of the use of narrow AI such as Siri in the iPhone. More narrow AIs will be developed in the near future, all of which will lead down the path to Artificial Intelligence in the future that will have the mental capacity of a human being. Projections for AI with human intelligence range from 2045 to the end of the century (Kurzweil, 2005).

> To maximize the potential of Artificial Intelligence and be truly digital leaders, companies must reimagine and reinvent their processes from scratch—and create self-adapting, self-optimizing "living processes" that use machine learning algorithms and real-time data to continuously improve. (Accenture Technology, 2018, p. 3)

Today's interaction involves humans helping to improve an algorithm's performance through activities like data-cleaning, and data- and image-labeling.

> Data-cleaning is . . . the process of detecting and correcting (or removing) corrupt or inaccurate records from a record set, table, or database and refers to identifying incomplete, incorrect, inaccurate or irrelevant parts of the data and then replacing, modifying, or deleting the dirty or coarse data. (Jimenez, 2017, p. 184)

On a higher level, humans are developing algorithms that mimic human behaviors to improve the Artificial Intelligence's social, emotional, and natural language intelligence. These improvements in Artificial Intelligence are increasingly noticed in more advanced robots such as Hanson Robotics' Sophia, The Robot. However, Sophia is still an example of narrow AI.

The digital twin application used at General Electric, originally developed by NASA as a way to manage assets, is yet another Artificial Intelligence concept that is currently being used. A digital twin is a functioning virtual copy of a company, or other industrial asset, that exists in the digital realm. It can simulate numerous scenarios in real time, ensuring that maintenance is based on need rather than on the calendar.

The digital twin captures the operating history of its physical twin, records key performance indicators (KPIs) to monitor present performance, and offers insights for the future to drive and predict business outcomes (Forbes, 2017). If this type of narrow Artificial Intelligence were used in education, it could personalize each student's curriculum, based on an individual's learning needs.

THE FUTURE OF ARTIFICIAL INTELLIGENCE

Artificial Intelligence and education are powerful tools that are inextricably intertwined now and in the future. "AIEd is also a powerful tool to open up what is sometimes called the 'black box of learning,' giving us deeper, and more fine-grained understandings of how learning actually happens" (Luckin et al., 2016, p. 18).

Artificial Intelligence is taking on more sophisticated roles within technological experiences, with the potential to make every interface both simple and smart—setting a high bar for how future interactions would work. Robots are currently working alongside people, and smart machines are performing triage in hospital settings in order to augment the clinician's decision making.

Contextual intelligence and deep-learning algorithms are raising the bar for transactions and interactions in many industries. Artificial Intelligence will play a primary role in making relationships stronger through new Artificial Intelligence–driven services that help curate, advise, and coordinate lifestyle and care for people (Accenture, 2017). As Artificial Intelligence becomes more sophisticated, it will increasingly become a partner with humans, supporting them in their daily lives.

ETHICS OF ARTIFICIAL INTELLIGENCE

Artificial Intelligence presents significant, unique ethical issues. Nick Bostrom is one of the leading researchers in the area of ethics and Artificial Intelligence. Bostrom finds that:

> ethical issues related to the possible future creation of machines with general intellectual capabilities far outstripping those of humans are quite distinct from any ethical problems arising in current automation and information systems. Such superintelligence would not be just another technological development; it would be the most important invention ever made, and would lead to explosive progress in all scientific and technological fields, as the superintelligence would conduct research with superhuman efficiency. (Bostrom, 2003, para. 1)

Bostrom presents a critical issue in the debate on ethics and Artificial Intelligence. He reflects on the notion that a Super Artificial Intelligence will exceed humans in ethical and moral thinking.

> To the extent that ethics is a cognitive pursuit, a superintelligence could also easily surpass humans in the quality of its moral thinking. However, it would be up to the designers of the superintelligence to specify its original motivations. Since the superintelligence may become unstoppably powerful because of its intellectual superiority and the technologies it could develop, it is crucial that it be provided with human-friendly motivations. (Bostrom, 2003, para. 1)

The discussion about "human-friendly motivation" is a concern when developing and understanding the algorithms of Artificial Intelligence (Bostrom, 2003, para. 1). Individuals working in Artificial Intelligence need to be able to offer simple explanations of the science of algorithms to non-technical professionals.

> People will direct and control artificial intelligence to fit their lifestyle and goals. The "black box" nature of machine-learning algorithms can cause concerns, especially when systems recommend or take actions that defy conventional wisdom. By using experimental analytical techniques on AI data models, humans can explain why algorithms make the decisions they do, such as passing over an employee for a promotion, halting a manufacturing process or targeting a subset of customers with online ads. Large companies that use advanced AI systems should consider hiring employees who can explain the inner workings of complex algorithms to non-technical professionals. (Accenture Technology, 2018, p. 12)

When IBM developed Watson, the company reviewed and considered the ethics research on the use of Artificial Intelligence. The question is, are they prepared to let that happen without proper debate or control? The ethics of AI, as written about extensively by the Oxford philosopher Nick Bostrom, need especially careful attention: "responsibility, transparency, auditability, incorruptibility, predictability [. . .]; all criteria that must be considered in an algorithm intended to replace human judgement of social functions (Luckin et al., 2016, p. 39).

IBM continues to have substantial reflection on the questions brought about by the use of Artificial Intelligence: "What are the implications of the methods, technologies, and ideologies that underpin the generation, analysis, interpretation, and use of AIEd system data? Who owns the data, who can use it, for what purposes, and who is ultimately accountable?" (Luckin et al., 2016, p. 39).

CHANGES IN ARTIFICIAL INTELLIGENCE

There are short-term, mid-term, and long-term expected changes that will occur in the field of Artificial Intelligence.

Short Term (1–5 Years)

"Today AI is used and developed for expert systems, research and simulation, image recognition, speech and natural language processing, autonomous systems such as self-driving cars and robots. It is also used for behavior modeling, personal recommendations, and input scoring" (Taglione, 2018, para. 14).

Robots who hold conversations with humans and experimental self-driving vehicles are the most popular advancements involving a high level of Artificial Intelligence. These two entities receive a vast amount of media attention, both causing excitement as well as certain reservations in today's society. While some are amused and excited about self-driving vehicles, others are cautious and skeptical, visualizing only the danger potential of this new technology.

Mid-Term (5–10 Years)

"If our emerging technology is going to merge humanity with the machine, augmenting our human intelligence with artificial intelligence, we need to manage the risk!" (Simpson, 2018, para. 12). Artificial Intelligence will continue to play a major role in many of the products people currently use today. The near future of Artificial Intelligence will increase the risk of isolation by making wireless devices more accessible, therefore expanding the use of social media in every aspect.

When one visits restaurants and events, it is noticeable that personal conversations are almost obsolete. Many families with young children have devices in one hand while eating dinner with the other. Live and open access to anything across the world deters families from having traditional discussion after school and work. Artificial Intelligence could possibly take this to the next level, causing conversation to be a lost art.

Well-designed systems can help society remove bias and promote diversity by creating screening tools that remove names, ethnicity, and gender orientation inquiries from various loan and employment applications. "If we use biased data to train our machine learning AI, then we get biased AI. The classical garbage in, garbage out problem" (Simpson, 2018, para. 6). Simpson notes that a female voice is used on most cell phones and other external home electronics, promoting the notion that personal assistants are predominately female. While this may be unintentional, it serves as an example of how society is influenced by outdated norms.

Long Term (10–20 Years)

"Robots are making healthcare services available 24/7, having AI nurses and caretakers monitoring a patient's at-home condition and prompting patients to take their medication" (Hyacinth, 2017, p. 27). In the future, this could help doctors spend more time discovering new drugs and treatments for patients while decreasing the number of deaths caused by overmedication or allergic reactions.

"Through data-driven algorithms, machines will be able to respond to heath concerns and even make diagnoses" (Hyacinth, 2017, p. 27). This is just one aspect of Artificial Intelligence that could boost the health-care industry while improving the quality of life for millions.

EFFECTS OF AI ON COMMUNITY COLLEGES AND UNIVERSITIES

Short Term (1–5 Years)

Though there are Artificial Intelligence applications in use in classrooms, it is not widespread. Short-term goals for Artificial Intelligence education applications should be to implement small changes that are widespread in community colleges and senior institutions.

> A multitude of AIEd-driven applications are already in use in our schools and universities. Many incorporate AIEd and educational data mining (EDM) techniques to "track" the behaviours of students—for example, collecting data on class attendance and assignment submission in order to identify (and provide support to) students at risk of abandoning their studies. (Luckin et al., 2016, p. 24)

Gopal Mohan, a robotics instructor at York Technical College, was asked where he sees Artificial Intelligence progressing in the near future within our education system. Mohan responded, "I see aspects of AI becoming most of the technical courses that students will be taking" (G. Mohan, personal communication, July 18, 2018).

Mid-Term (5–10 Years)

Artificial Intelligence is linked to many other technological fields. Community colleges and senior institutions not only need to offer more courses in Artificial Intelligence, but also to understand the importance of AI in education as the field expands. Mohan was asked what he sees is the importance of Artificial Intelligence in education for our future students. He responded, "Our graduates find employment in high-tech industries. Knowledge of AI practices helps them to navigate and progress through the developments in the various fields including drone technology and IOT (Internet of Things)" (G. Mohan, personal communication, July 18, 2018).

Long Term (10–20 Years)

IBM, in its Artificial Intelligence education software application, is focusing on three areas of future development: "we focus on three categories of AIEd software applications that have been designed to support learning most directly: personal tutors for every learner, intelligent support for collaborative learning, and intelligent virtual reality" (Luckin et al., 2016, p. 24).

One of IBM's long-term goals for Watson is to provide tutors for every student.

> Unfortunately, one-to-one tutoring is untenable for all students. Not only will there never be enough human tutors; it would also never be affordable. All of this begs the question: how can we make the positive impact of one-to-one tutoring available to all learners across all subjects? (Luckin et al., 2016, p. 24)

IBM has developed a system for tutoring that is being continuously revised and brought up-to-date as new software and technologies are created.

> This is where Intelligent Tutoring Systems (ITS) come in. ITS use AI techniques to simulate one-to-one human tutoring, delivering learning activities best matched to a learner's cognitive needs and providing targeted and timely feedback, all without an individual teacher having to be present. Some ITS put the learner in control of their own learning in order to help students develop self-regulation skills; others use pedagogical strategies to scaffold learning so that the learner is appropriately challenged and supported. (Luckin et al., 2016, p. 24)

ADVICE TO ADMINISTRATORS IN COMMUNITY COLLEGES AND UNIVERSITIES

Short Term (1–5 Years)

IBM's research into Artificial Intelligence in education understands that "AIEd needs to begin with the pedagogy and be more ambitious!" (Luckin et al., 2016, p. 51). IBM affirms that teachers will be vital to Artificial Intelligence education in the future. It is necessary that faculty begin to understand their role, purpose, and how they will complement artificial intelligence education.

> We are in no doubt that teachers need to be central agents in the next phase of AIEd. In one sense this is obvious—it is teachers who will be the orchestrators of when, and how, to use these AIEd tools. In turn, the AIEd tools, and the data driven insights that these tools provide, will empower teachers to decide how best to marshal the various resources at their disposal. (Luckin et al., 2016, p. 31)

Mid-Term (5–10 Years)

The use of AI in education needs to be present in the discussion of development and creation of future education initiatives. It is important to recognize the initial fears faculty and administration have about including Artificial Intelligence in the classroom.

> Most schools of education around the world are not equipped—or not interested—in this debate. They either ignore this conversation, or simply attack the entire enterprise of AI in education—but these attacks are not stopping wide dissemination of various types of AIED projects in schools, mainly driven by corporations and fueled by incentives that might not work in the benefit of students (i.e., massive cost reduction, deprofessionalization of teachers, additional standardization of content and instruction). (Rosé et al., 2018, p. XIV)

IBM is part of the voice that is presenting Artificial Intelligence education positively and explaining the benefits of the use of Artificial Intelligence in classrooms and other learning environments.

> In this scenario, the academic AIED community has a crucial responsibility—it could be the only voice capable to steering the debate, and the technology, towards more productive paths. This talk will be about the hard choices that AIED needs to face in the coming years, reviewing the history of AI in education, its promise, and possible futures. (Rosé et al., 2018, p. XIV)

IBM is already reacting to the debates, and answering the questions about Artificial Intelligence in education and the issues this subject presents:

> Should we focus on technologies that promote student agency and curricular flexibility, or on making sure everyone learns the same? How do we tackle new learning environments such as makerspaces and other inquiry-driven spaces? What is the role of physical science labs versus virtual, AI-driven labs? How can AIED impact—positively and negatively—equity in education? (Rosé et al., 2018, p. XIV)

Long Term (10–20 Years)

Artificial Intelligence and Artificial Intelligence education are inseparably linked.

Moreover, industry needs, and workforce development are interlinked with Artificial Intelligence education. In the long term, community colleges and senior institutions need to be aware of the Artificial Intelligence needs of industry, and how instruction and training can be improved to meet these needs.

The future of AIEd is inextricably linked to the future of AI. The increasing consumerization of AI technologies brings with it a massive increase in the number of people who are developing AI. The pace of innovation and development in general is at its fastest rate ever and the current popularity of AI should mean that innovation in AIEd is a focus of attention for an increasing number of businesses. (Luckin et al., 2016, p. 33)

ADVICE TO STUDENTS IN COMMUNITY COLLEGES AND SENIOR INSTITUTIONS

Student input is necessary for the development and creation of Artificial Intelligence in general and AI programs at community colleges and universities. IBM includes students and parents in the development of Artificial Intelligence Education Systems. "Involve teachers, students, and parents to ensure that future AIEd systems meet their needs (a participatory design process that will lead to better AIEd products, to teachers more knowledgeable about the processes of learning, and to more successful learners)" (Luckin et al., 2016, p. 55).

Carnegie Mellon University is a leading senior institution in the development of Artificial Intelligence programs. Andrew Moore, the dean of the School of Computer Science at Carnegie Mellon University, stated, "Specialists in artificial intelligence have never been more important, in shorter supply or in greater demand by employers" (Spice, 2018, para. 3).

In the fall of 2018, Carnegie Mellon University will have the first Artificial Intelligence degree offered by a United States university. This degree was created "in response to extraordinary technical breakthroughs in AI and the growing demand by students and employers for training that prepares people for careers in AI" (Spice, 2018, para. 2).

CONCLUSION

Artificial Intelligence is becoming an integral part of society. It is expected that the upward trend in capabilities of AI will continue, and eventually assist society in a multitude of computations. The psychological and emotional repercussions of introducing Artificial Intelligence into society is concerning.

The continuous growth of Artificial Intelligence will be contingent on society's ethical opinion concerning three major factors, which are: the benefits and tolerability of Artificial Intelligence, businesses gaining competitive advantages from using Artificial Intelligence, and sustained funding for research and development of Artificial Intelligence. In the future, as humanity increasingly works together with Artificial Intelligence to change the world, the workforce will need to engage in lifelong learning and developing the skills necessary to keep abreast with the rapid changes that will occur.

CHAPTER SUMMARY

- Currently Artificial Intelligence consists of very powerful computers that can accomplish specific tasks.
- Both Deep Blue and Watson are examples of narrow AI.
- Projections for artificial intelligence with a human intelligence range from 2045 to the end of the century.
- Artificial Intelligence and education are powerful tools that are inextricably intertwined now and in the future.
- Robots are currently working alongside people, and smart machines are preforming triage in hospital settings in order to augment the clinician's decision making.
- Artificial intelligence presents significant, unique ethical issues.
- Individuals working in Artificial Intelligence need to be able to offer simple explanations of the science of algorithms to non-technical professionals.
- Robots who hold conversations with humans and experimental self-driving vehicles are the most popular advancements involving a high level of artificial intelligence.
- When one visits restaurants and events, it is noticeable that personal conversations are almost obsolete.
- Although there are artificial intelligent applications in use in the classroom, it is not widespread.
- Artificial Intelligence is linked to many other technological fields.
- Community colleges and universities need to not only offer more courses in Artificial Intelligence, but also understand the importance of AI in education as the field expands.
- IBM has developed a system for tutoring that is being continuously revised and brought up-to-date as new software and technologies are created.
- IBM affirms that teachers will be vital to Artificial Intelligence education in the future.
- It is important to recognize the initial fears faculty and administration have about including artificial intelligence in the classroom.
- Artificial Intelligence and Artificial Intelligence education are inseparably linked.
- Student input is necessary for the development and creation of Artificial Intelligence in general and AI programs in community colleges and universities.
- In the fall of 2018, Carnegie Mellon University will have the first Artificial Intelligence degree by a United States university.
- Artificial intelligence is becoming an integral part of society.

REFERENCES

Accenture. (2017, May 30). Technology for people. Retrieved July 14, 2018, from https://www.accenture.com/t20180425T033207Z__w__/us-en/_acnmedia/PDF-45/Accenture-Digital-Health-Technology-Vision-2017.pdf#zoom=50.

Accenture Technology. (2018, April 20). Process reimagined. Retrieved July 14, 2018, from https://www.accenture.com/t20180424T033337Z__w__/us-en/_acnmedia/PDF-76/Accenture-Process-Reimagined.pdf#zoom=50.

Baker, S. (2011). *Final jeopardy: Man vs. machine and the quest to know everything.* New York: Houghton Mifflin Harcourt.

Bostrom, N. (2003). Ethical issues in advanced artificial intelligence. Retrieved June 16, 2018, from https://nickbostrom.com/ethics/ai.html.

Forbes, A. (2017, October 30). Time to befriend the digital twins. Retrieved July 16, 2018, from https://www.ge.com/power/transform/article.transform.articles.2017.oct.time-to-befriend-the-digital-t.

Hyacinth, B. T. (2017). *The future of leadership: Rise of automation, robotics and artificial Intelligence.* Brigette Tasha Hyacinth.

Jimenez, F. (2017). *Intelligent vehicles enabling technologies and future developments.* San Diego: Elsevier Science.

Kasparov, G. (2017). *Deep thinking: Where machine intelligence ends and human creativity begins.* New York: Perseus Books, LLC.

Kurzweil, R. (2005). *The singularity is near: When humans transcend biology.* New York: Penguin Books.

Luckin, R., Holmes, W., Griffiths, M., & Forcier, L. (2016). Intelligence unleashed—An argument for AI in education. Retrieved June 19, 2018, from https://www.bing.com/cr?IG=AF870C386C8545BA901147ADFF9AD4A4&CID=3DB72648167F6E8539032A7F17826F61&rd=1&h=sUul0kExeNjHd3ZnC5jbozh-U37at9md8-fKwVaT5i0&v=1&r=https://www.pearson.com/content/dam/corporate/global/pearson-dot-com/files/innovation/Intelligence-Unleashed-Publication.pdf&p=DevEx.LB.1,5560.1.

Rosé, C. P., Martinez-Maldonado, R., Hoppe, H. U., Luckin, R., Mavrikis, M., Porayska-Pomsta, K., & Du Boulay, B. (Eds.). (2018). *Artificial intelligence in education: 19th international conference, AIED 2018, London, UK, June 27–30, 2018: Proceedings Part 1.* Cham, CH: Springer.

Simpson, G. (2018, May 16). The societal impact of AI. Retrieved July 20, 2018, from https://www.cio.com/article/3273565/artificial-intelligence/the-societal-impact-of-ai.html.

Spice, B. (2018, May 10). Carnegie Mellon launches undergraduate degree in artificial intelligence. Retrieved June 25, 2018, from https://www.cs.cmu.edu/news/carnegie-mellon-launches-undergraduate-degree-artificial-intelligence.

Taglione, J. (2018, May 18). AI: Where we are now, and the short-term problems—The Startup—Medium. Retrieved July 16, 2018, from https://medium.com/swlh/ai-where-we-are-now-and-the-short-term-problems-cfe2e41cc5e2.

Chapter Nine

Nanotechnology

Kira Ferris and Dahmon King

Nanoscience is a field of study concerned with manipulation of matter on the anatomic, molecular, and supra-molecular scale. Nanotechnology refers to the application of nanoscience for building nano-components based on the manipulation of matter with at least one dimension sized from 1 to 100 nanometers (Internet of Nanoscale Things, 2017).

The National Nanotechnology Initiative is a United States Government research and development initiative involving nanotechnology-related activities of twenty departments and independent agencies. This initiative describes nanotechnology as "science, engineering, and technology conducted at the nanoscale, about 1 to 100 nanometers" (Slingerland, 2016, p. 7). For years, scientists have been creating and manipulating extremely tiny materials, atom by atom, in specialized clean rooms. Formerly, a Ph.D. was needed to be able to enter the field of nanoscience (Argonne National Laboratory, 2017).

Nanotechnology is now a megatrend that impacts science, technology, and daily life. Though nanotechnology can be viewed as a fairly new concept, it has existed for at least 1,600 years. As reported in *Smithsonian* magazine regarding the glass chalice known as the Lycurgus Cup, the Romans

> impregnated the glass with particles of silver and gold, ground down until they were as small as 50 nanometers in diameter, less than one-thousandth the size of a grain of table salt. The exact mixture of the precious metals suggests the Romans knew what they were doing. (Merali, 2013, para. 2)

Richard Feynman is credited as the individual who introduced the world to nanotechnology in his December 1959 talk entitled "There's Plenty of Room at the Bottom." Almost forty years later, another scientist, Richard

Errett Smalley, would push nanotechnology into the spotlight once again, stating that "nanotechnology is the builder's final frontier" (Schummer & Baird, 2006, p. 335). Smalley was a 1996 Nobel laureate in chemistry and was honored by the United States Senate in a resolution that named him the Father of Nanotechnology.

This chapter explores nanotechnology by providing an overview of the discipline, insight into the current situation, the future of nanotechnology, the ethics of nanotechnology, changes in nanotechnology, the effects of nanotechnology on community colleges and senior institutions, and advice for administration, faculty, and students.

THE CURRENT SITUATION OF NANOTECHNOLOGY

When discussing the current state of nanotechnology, Elie Azzi, a research associate at the Joint School of Nanoscience and Nanoengineering, said, "Embrace the change, it's here" (E. Azzi, personal communication, June 1, 2018). Today the field of nanotechnology spans across multiple disciplines: "Nanotechnology will have a profound impact on our economy and society; it is a modern industrial revolution. Nanotechnology represents a megatrend, bringing disruptive innovation. It has become a general-purpose technology, being applicable across various industrial sectors" (Winkelmann and Bhushan, 2016, loc. 223).

Today, high school students can explore the field of nanoscience thanks to many partnerships with different corporations throughout the world. High school students can get a hands-on introduction to nanoscience by growing copper wires at the nano-scale (one billionth of a meter) and the micro-scale (one millionth of a meter) using technology developed at Argonne's Center for Nanoscale Materials (Argonne National Laboratory, 2017).

There are several colleges and universities that offer a variety of programs in the field of nanoscience. Nanotechnology can encompass a vast number of disciplines, including chemistry, biology, physics, materials science, and engineering. At the Joint School of Nanoscience and Nanoengineering in Greensboro, North Carolina, the research program focuses on several sectors of nanotechnology. These sectors are nanobioscience, nanometrology, nanomaterials, nanobioelectronics, nanoenergy, and computational nanotechnology (E. Azzi, personal communication, June 1, 2018).

Nanoparticles are used as additives in products such as motor oil, sunscreen, deodorant, and cosmetics. These are just a few common household products derived from the field of nanotechnology. Electronics such as cell phones, computers, and video games also contain millions of nanoscale components in the form of transistors.

Commonly known as nanoelectronics, this technology might increase the capabilities of electronic devices while reducing their weight and power consumption. This can be accomplished by decreasing the weight and thickness of the screens, increasing the density of memory chips, and reducing the size of transistors used in integrated circuits.

> Large-scale nanomanufacturing processes that produce quality nanomaterials are still being researched and developed. These processes fall into two categories. Top-down approaches start with full-sized materials and break them down into nano sizes. The making of computer components falls in this category. By contrast, bottom-up approaches build material at an atomic or molecular level, often employing complicated chemical processes to result in the desired materials. (Slingerland, 2016, p. 12)

THE FUTURE OF NANOTECHNOLOGY

The future of nanotechnology has unlimited possibilities and applications. When debating the future of nanotechnology, Elie Azzi highlights that "What holds us back is the consumer psyche and the FDA" (E. Azzi, personal communication, June 1, 2018).

The future of nanotechnology is an active topic of discussion among researchers, environmentalists, industrialists, technologists, engineers, and people in the health industry. In the future, nanotechnology may be used in producing more efficient delivery systems of vaccines and other prescription drugs, in improving imaging agents for medical analysis, and in new cancer treatments that are able to target specific cells. Environmental applications could improve energy efficiency, reduce the use of some solvents and waste products, desalinate water for drinking, and monitor contaminants in a variety of applications.

As is the case with any new technology, many health and environmental effects of nanotechnology are unknown. The most common nanomaterials are found in silver, carbon, titanium, silicon/silica, and zinc. Nanoscale materials display a very large surface area per unit of mass, making some of them particularly reactive.

These materials may also have different optical, magnetic, or electrical properties than their conventional counterparts. Among the physical characteristics raising questions are their capacity to integrate into biological systems, change cell metabolism, and evade biological defense mechanisms in the body. More research needs to be done in this area to determine the best uses for nanotechnology.

THE ETHICS OF NANOTECHNOLOGY

The rapidly growing field of nanotechnology and its products poses new and interesting challenges to environmental policymakers and institutions. With nanotechnology covering a wide scope of applications, ranging from gene therapy and drug delivery to water treatment, ethics must be paramount in discussions. There are too many avenues for illegal use and reckless practices. Scientists and students who will use nanotechnology for various processes should feel compelled to comply with the ethics outlined by a corporation or educational institution.

"It would be difficult to deny the potential benefits of nanotechnology and stop development of research related to it since it has already begun to penetrate many different fields of research" (Chen, 2002, para. 16). Andrew Chen, in his article "The Ethics of Nanotechnology," says, "The two greatest threats from development of nanotechnology are catastrophic accidents and misuse" (Chen, 2002, para. 14).

Chen identifies professional, legal, policy, and ethical issues in nanotechnology. These issues include undetectable surveillance, development of policies that cover the many fields of nanotechnology, and the research agenda of those who control nanotechnology funding (Chen, 2002, para. 15).

CHANGES IN NANOTECHNOLOGY

There are short-term, mid-term, and long-term expected changes that will occur in the field of nanotechnology.

Short Term (1–5 Years)

In the short term, "We will see small introductions, especially in the construction of everyday electronics" (E. Azzi, personal communication, June 1, 2018). Dr. Bernadette T. Donovan-Merkert, director of the Nanoscale Science Ph.D. Program at the University of North Carolina–Charlotte, presents a similar sentiment regarding materials for constructing products: "We will see new materials, materials that are lighter, stronger, and more durable" (B. Donovan-Merkert, personal communication, June 15, 2018).

Mid-Term (5–10 Years)

In looking at mid-term changes in nanotechnology, Donovan-Merkert sees "advances in the areas of detection and treatment of diseases" (B. Donovan-Merkert, personal communication, June 15, 2018). Azzi reflected the same response: "We see advancement in the Tesla cars, and in medicine, especially drug delivery and personalized medicine" (E. Azzi, personal communication, June 1, 2018).

Long Term (10–20 Years)

In the long term, changes in nanotechnology can be seen in "ultradense computer memory, and sensing applications for agricultural, biological, chemical, and homeland security applications" (B. Donovan-Merkert, personal communication, June 1, 2018). In the future, "education programs must adapt to enable the new generations of nanotechnology methods and products, as well as to the increasingly science and engineering convergence trends" (Winkelmann and Bhushan, 2016, loc. 57).

Nanotechnology is the current and future basis of many materials, concepts, and technologies.

> Nanoscale science and engineering will increasingly integrate with other knowledge and technology domains in a variety of applications. Convergence between key technologies subsequently leads to bifurcation into new emerging technology platforms. Nanotechnology development between about 2000 and 2030 may be seen as a convergence–divergence process for science and technology megatrends. (Winkelmann and Bhushan, 2016, loc. 64)

The pyramid below shows how the technologies in this book are built upon each other. There needs to be advancements in nanotechnologies to have ensuing advancements in the other fields. Articles that illustrate the relationship between nanotechnology and the subsequent topics in this book can be found in the reference section of this chapter.

THE EFFECTS OF NANOTECHNOLOGY ON COMMUNITY COLLEGES AND SENIOR INSTITUTIONS

There are short-term, mid-term, and long-term effects of nanotechnology on community colleges and senior institutions.

Short Term (1–5 Years)

We will first "likely see an increase in the presence of nanotechnology education, but this could take many forms—research, programs, courses, modified courses" (B. Donovan-Merkert, personal communication, June 15, 2018).

Five areas have been identified where nanotechnology education development is needed. They are "interdisciplinary education; K–12 education, excitement, and creativity; vocational, undergraduate, graduate, and continuing

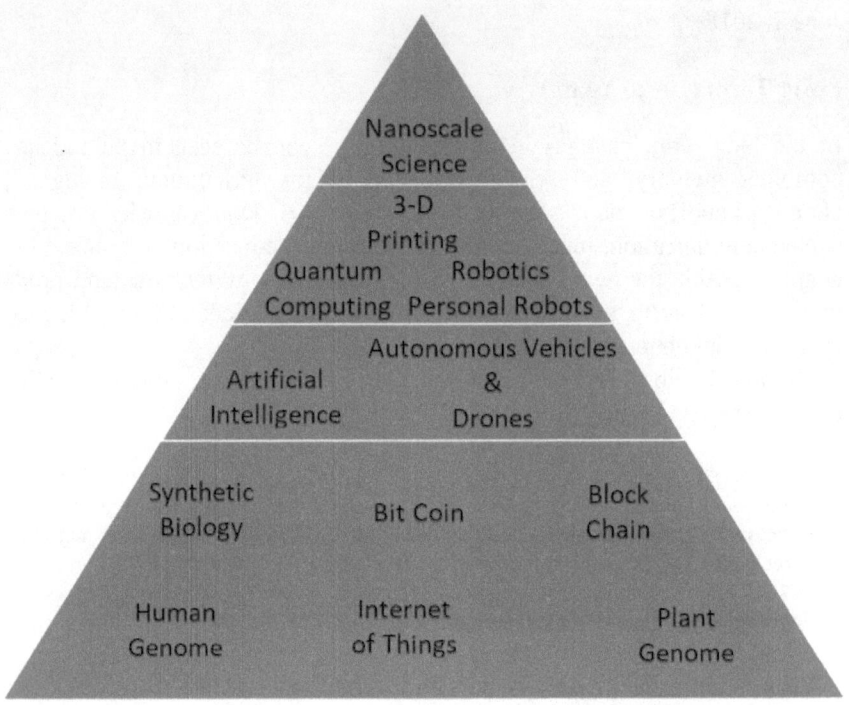

Figure 9.1. Pyramid Build of Exponential Technologies. Pyramid depicting the scale of exponential technologies in this book. Figure design by Kira Davad Ferris.

education programs; educator training; and informal science education" (Winkelmann and Bhushan, 2016, loc. 742).

Mid-Term (5–10 Years)

Issues of low student recruitment can be a challenge for nanotechnology programs.

> Many high school students with an interest in science or nanotechnology are already on a path to attend a university and may not have much interest in a 2-year degree. Even though the content and breadth of the "nanoscience" experience in these 2-year programs is often stronger than what is covered within a single major at a university, there is still a hesitation regarding an AAS degree. (Winkelmann and Bhushan, 2016, loc. 7,588)

Long Term (10–20 Years)

Research has demonstrated the need for individuals with varying education levels to fill the employment needs of nanotechnology.

> From a demand standpoint, multiple studies have shown a forecasted need for millions of nano knowledgeable employees—not only at a PhD level but with hundreds of thousands employees needed at the technician level. Many community colleges are stepping up to the challenge of filling this need. (Winkelmann and Bhushan, 2016, loc. 7,536)

ADVICE FOR ADMINISTRATORS IN COMMUNITY COLLEGES AND SENIOR INSTITUTIONS

Administrators and faculty need to recognize that

> successful implementation of nanoscience content is dependent on five factors. These factors are administrative support, faculty awareness, knowledge and interest, local industry support, facilities, and student recruitment and retention. One of the most critical factors of success is the support of local industry and meeting the needs of that local industry. (Winkelmann and Bhushan, 2016, loc. 7,652)

Donovan-Merkert offers a list of suggestions for administrators and faculty of community colleges and senior institutions. This advice includes:

- administrators who work collaboratively with the faculty;
- asking the faculty what they need to educate students about nanotechnology, and not launching new initiatives without first consulting with the faculty, who will ultimately be responsible for delivering the education to the students;
- not having institutions bring nanotechnology to students in the same way, and allowing some institutions the funding needed to purchase equipment and hire technical staff: think about what your institution is capable of doing, and what it should do;
- partnering with faculty in developing a vision for nanotechnology education, including the resources needed, such as facilities and faculty development;
- providing resources needed, and working with the faculty to acquire resources needed for nanotechnology education: the resources needed will vary by institution; and
- using the faculty to assess student needs and develop courses, curricula, and internships that support the shared vision for nanotechnology education (B. Donovan-Merkert, personal communication, June 15, 2018).

Short Term (1–5 Years)

The nanotechnology industry needs graduates from community colleges and senior institutions: "First, industry needed employees of all levels, not just PhDs, who knew how to operate the family of nanoscience tools, such as Atomic Force Microscopes (AFMs), Scanning Electron Microscopes (SEMs), Raman spectrometers and Tunneling Electron Microscopes (TEMs)" (Winkelmann and Bhushan, 2016, loc. 7,551).

In one case study, results showed that employers not only wanted employees who knew how to use nanoscale tools, but also who understood the reasoning and concepts behind nanoscale technology.

> [They] . . . wanted employees that not only knew how to operate the tools of nanoscience, the employers wanted employees that understand the concepts behind the equipment operation and measurement and also understand the fundamental concepts of the nanoscale world. These concepts include sense of scale, atomic and molecular structure, surface area and chemical reactivity, and material properties at the nanoscale. Gaining this understanding also requires aspects of physics, chemistry, biology and materials science. (Winkelmann and Bhushan, 2016, loc. 7,553)

Mid-Term (5–10 Years)

Mid-term advice for administrators and faculty focuses on being patient in the development of nanotechnology programs.

> Many emerging technology programs, especially those as new as nanotechnology, require a substantial period of time to get students interested and invested and the program. This requires that the administration be patient with the growth of the program or courses. Faculty involvement is critical especially in multidisciplinary programs such as nanotechnology. (Winkelmann and Bhushan, 2016, loc. 7,662)

Long Term (10–20 Years)

The long-term outlook for nanotechnology programs is the continued development of programs. "Curricula focusing on nanoscience and nanotechnology should continue to be developed for various levels. These levels include 2-year vocational programs, traditional 4-year university and graduate education programs, and continuing education for practicing professionals" (Winkelmann and Bhushan, 2016, loc. 742).

ADVICE TO STUDENTS IN COMMUNITY COLLEGES AND SENIOR INSTITUTIONS

Education is essential for students in the field of nanotechnology. Education and training are essential to produce a new generation of scientists, engineers, and skilled workers with the flexible and interdisciplinary Research and Development (R&D) approach necessary for rapid progress in nanosciences and nanotechnology. A trained nanotechnology workforce at both vocational and professional levels needs to be developed. This needs to be accomplished with both formal and informal education efforts, starting with the foundations in children and increasing in technical and specialized education through the university and continuing education levels (Winkelmann and Bhushan, 2016, loc. 709).

Donovan-Merkert offers advice to students interested in entering the field of nanotechnology. This advice includes:

- learning as much science and math as you can;
- becoming an expert in conducting laboratory procedures, and collecting, recording, and interpreting data;
- making sure you understand everything you do in the laboratory, and why you are doing it—internships and undergraduate research are great ways to acquire this expertise;
- becoming an expert in how relevant scientific instruments operate, and the types of information that can be obtained from specific instruments; and
- having a strong technical background is only part of the picture; employers, and graduate and professional schools also want students to be self-motivated, good critical thinkers, good communicators (orally and in writing), and good team players (B. Donovan-Merkert, personal communication, June 15, 2018).

The emphasis on soft skills is important, and it is found that

> companies need employees that can communicate (oral and written), analyze data, work in a team environment, understand critical thinking and knowledge transfer and have attributes such as innovation, creativity, lifelong learning and so on. Teaching these skills does not happen in just one or two classes but these skills and attributes are integrated into all of the courses across the program. (Winkelmann and Bhushan, 2016, loc. 7,567)

CONCLUSION

As nanotechnology evolves throughout every industry, it is important for those involved in the short-term, mid-term, and long-term growth to place considerable attention on safety, education, and ethics. Closely monitoring and growing the vast uses of nanotechnology can bring us toward the next industrial revolution. Further research and funding will assist colleges, universities, and corporations toward advances in the field of nanotechnology. Nanotechnology is an essential aspect of the development of most products that are used today.

CHAPTER SUMMARY

- Nanotechnology is a megatrend that will impact science, technology, and daily life.
- Today the field of nanotechnology spans across multiple disciplines.
- Currently high school students can explore the field of nano science thanks to many partnerships with the different corporations throughout the world.
- Nanoparticles are used as additives in products such as motor oil, sunscreen, deodorant, and cosmetics.
- The future of nanotechnology is an active topic of discussion among researchers, environmentalists, industrialists, technologists, engineers, and people in the health-care industry.
- Most nano materials are found in silver, carbon, titanium, silicone/silica, and zinc.
- A rapidly growing field of nanotechnology and its products poses new and interesting challenges to environmental policymakers and institutions.
- In the next five years, small introductions in the construction of everyday electronics will be seen.
- In the long term, changes in nanotechnology will be seen in ultra-dense computer memory, and sensing applications for agriculture, biology, chemistry, and homeland security.
- In the next five to ten years, nanotechnology will be appearing in all levels of education from K–12 through graduate school.
- In the long term, research has demonstrated the need for individuals with varying educational levels to fill the employment needs of nanotechnology.
- Administrators in higher education will need to become aware of the impact of nanotechnology on education.
- The nanotechnology industry needs graduates from community colleges and senior institutions.
- Education is essential for students in the field of nanotechnology.
- Students should become aware of the nanotechnology field and understand the courses in science and math they will need to take.
- In addition, soft skills will be extremely important.

- Nanotechnology will demand considerable attention in the areas of safety, education, and ethics.

REFERENCES

Argonne National Laboratory. (2017, August 18). Nanotechnology moves from the clean room to the classroom. States News Service. Retrieved July 17, 2018, from http://www.highbeam.com/doc/1G1-501026372.html?refid=easy_hf.

Chen, A. (2002, March 3). The ethics of nanotechnology. Retrieved June 20, 2018, from https://www.scu.edu/ethics/focus-areas/technology-ethics/resources/the-ethics-of-nanotechnology/.

Internet of Nanoscale Things: Global nano iot market outlook and forecasts report 2017–2022—Research and Markets. (2017, March 09). Retrieved July 18, 2018, from https://www.businesswire.com/news/home/20170309005631/en/Internet-Nanoscale-Things-Global-Nano-IoT-Market.

Merali, Z. (2013, September 01). This 1,600-year-old goblet shows that the Romans were nanotechnology pioneers. Retrieved June 20, 2018, from https://www.smithsonianmag.com/history/this-1600-year-old-goblet-shows-that-the-romans-were-nanotechnology-pioneers-787224/.

Schummer, J., and Baird, D. (2006). *Nanotechnology challenges: Implications for philosophy, ethics and society*. Hackensack, NJ: World Scientific Pub.

Slingerland, J. (2016). *Nanotechnology*. Minneapolis, MN: Essential Library, Abdo Publishing.

Winkelmann, K., & Bhushan, B. (Eds.). (2016). *Global perspectives of nanoscience and engineering education*. S.l.: Springer Nature. doi:10.1007/978-3-319-31833-2.

Chapter Ten

Quantum Computing

Darrel W. Staat

CLASSICAL COMPUTERS

During the second decade of the twenty-first century, computers operate daily using silicon chips holding the equivalent of billions of transistors. These machines work well for a grand variety of jobs and projects for business, education, health, military, personal, and many other uses. The speed and accuracy of computers have increased exponentially over the years. In 1957, the first transistor was produced, and in 2018, the equivalent of 30 billion transistors rests within a silicon chip the size of a human fingernail.

QUANTUM COMPUTERS

The increase in computer power created by Moore's Law, the doubling of computer power every eighteen months, has created the digital world of today. What could be better? What is next in the computing world? Simply stated, quantum computing. This method of computing does not use silicon chips or transistors of any kind. It uses atoms and subatomic particles. It ventures into the quantum world, one that does not follow the rules of the universe thought to be normal and fitting well within the laws enunciated by Isaac Newton. Rather, it literally throws Newton's laws out the window and replaces them with the laws of quantum physics.

> Entering the realm of atoms opens up powerful new possibilities in the shape of quantum computing, with processors that could work millions of times faster than the ones we use today. Sounds amazing, but the trouble is that quantum computing is hugely more complex than traditional computing and operates in the *Alice in Wonderland* world of quantum physics, where the

"classical," sensible, everyday laws of physics no longer apply. Quantum computing means storing and processing information using individual atoms, ions, electrons, or photons. (Woodford, 2018)

Using atoms, which can be in two places at the same time, allows for phenomenal increased speed in processing. Rather than using bits, ones and twos, as takes place in today's classical computers, the quantum computer uses quantum bits, or "qubits," to process information. Without getting into the technical physics of the process, quantum computing makes all the increase in speed that classical computers using silicon chips have had powered by Moore's Law look like they are going in reverse. For those interested in the details of how quantum computers work, there is more than sufficient information on the internet.

Quantum computer power grows as the number of qubits used increases. For example:

> IBM's current cloud accessible quantum computer is built with 5 qubits, meaning it effectively has the computing power of 32 traditional bits. With 16 qubits, the new version has the equivalent of 65,536 bits, which allow for more complicated experiments to be run by developers and researchers through the cloud. The significant engineering improvements announced today will allow IBM to scale future processors to include 50 or more qubits, and demonstrate computer capabilities beyond today's classical computing systems. (Irving, May 18, 2017)

There is an interesting thing that happens when working with atoms; the temperature has to be close to absolute zero, 459.67 degrees below zero Fahrenheit. Further, the atoms will become unsecure if that temperature is not stable. One invention created to solve this problem is a "refrigerator" to keep things cool, developed by a team at Aalto University in Helsinki, Finland. It is a "chip containing two superconducting oscillators, connected to quantum-circuit refrigerators that use tunneling electrons to reduce energy and cool down the systems" (Irving, M. May 9, 2017). Seems appropriate, given the climate in Finland.

IBM has been working on a quantum computer and has created one that is accessible to researchers through the cloud. "Dubbed IBM Quantum Experience, this will provide users with the ability to experiment with individual quantum bits (qubits), process their own experiments, and run some of their own algorithms directly on IBM's quantum processor" (Jeffrey, May 5, 2016). This is a beginning that undoubtedly will expand as the years go by. A full-blown quantum computer of 500 qubits is most likely possible in about a decade.

As the quantum computer reaches maturity in the twenty-first century, digital opportunities beyond current thinking will become normal.

Computer World noted that the threat of quantum computing is already severe enough to prompt the U.S. National Security Agency to begin setting new standards for the next generation of encryption defenses. In a guide published in January, the agency advises operators of national security systems (NSS) of the need to "transition to quantum resistant algorithms in the future." (Smith, 2016)

There is good reason for the United States to be concerned about quantum computing. Other developed countries are working to develop successful quantum computers. China is investing some $10 billion in a four-million-square-foot facility to research quantum computing and quantum metrology. It is critical to be first in the race to develop quantum computing as it will make today's classical computers obsolete.

QUANTUM COMPUTING AND HIGHER EDUCATION

Although courses and programs on quantum computing are offered at extremely few community colleges and universities in the United States, many foreign countries are in full swing. In the United States, almost thirty universities are known to have quantum computing courses or programs. Some of the major universities include Harvard; California Institute of Technology; Massachusetts Institute of Technology; University of California–Berkeley; Stanford University; University of Colorado–Boulder; University of Maryland–College Park; University of California–Santa Barbara; University of Chicago; Yale University; Cal Tech; Princeton University; Southern Illinois University; Michigan State University, and others.

To see that major universities across the nation are already into the subject of quantum computing is encouraging. The Defense Advanced Research Projects Agency (DARPA) is a federal agency supporting research into quantum computing. It is critical that the United States get deeply involved in the topic of quantum computing as the power of that computing system is far beyond anything currently in existence. The military defense capabilities of the United States depend on computers, so it is critical that the military is well supported in the race to become the first to complete the capability to produce and use quantum computing.

D-WAVE

One company, D-Wave, which is located in Canada but works closely with American firms, has developed one type of quantum computer using a process called annealing. D-Wave's systems can be thought of as a large collection of magnets, each of which can flip orientations. These aren't qubits in the same way that the components of IBM or Intel's quantum processors are, but they do rely on quantum behavior for performing calculations. D-Wave's current system scales this (the number of magnets) up to 2,048 individual magnets, along with associated control hardware that determines which of these magnets is connected and how strong that connection is (Timmer, 2018).

Although this is a type of quantum computing, there are other methods under development, as well. No doubt considerable research along with trial and error will be conducted in the development of quantum computing before a standard is accepted by all concerned. For those interested quantum computing, follow-up research is critical to understanding its development.

CHINA'S QUANTUM SATELLITE

China launched the world's first quantum satellite in 2016. Its goal was to successfully send quantum encrypted messages from a height of 500 kilometers, some 310 miles, using a beam of entangled photons. Currently the quantum communications distance record on the earth is about 100 kilometers (62 miles) (Jeffery, August 18, 2016). "Quantum key encryption is quickly becoming an established method of ultra-secure communication, particularly as any attempt to intercept or read the encoded information means that the quantum state of the key will immediately collapse and render the data unreadable" (Jeffery, August 18, 2016, p. 2).

In other words, there must be the same digital key that is used to send and receive the information. Any other attempt to read the communication destroys it. Add to that the phenomenal speed at which the communication travels, and there is little time to intercept it, even if it could be read.

THE TIME FRAME FOR QUANTUM COMPUTING

The development of quantum computing will take some time. Current estimates are that it will take until about 2030 for a practical quantum computer to be on the market. However, since most developed countries are conducting research in the field, the opportunity for more rapid development is very possible. The United States, with the National Quantum Initiative Act of 2018, will bring encouragement, support, and funding to bear on the critical research. China and the UK are putting great emphasis and significant funding to support the development of quantum computing. Perhaps in the near future, many countries will form research consortia to help this technology develop.

Whatever the situation, quantum computing is here to stay. It will, when successfully developed, change the way in which communication will be handled. Those countries with the technology in full operation will have tremendous power and capabilities over those who do not. This is a race in which coming in first is critical.

ADVICE TO HIGHER EDUCATION ADMINISTRATORS

It seems to be obvious that administrators and faculty in community colleges and universities should be very interested in quantum computing. Internally it has the potential to change the way information will be communicated. Since almost every program offered in higher education has some computer activity within it, this new form will not only be interesting but will have an impact on how teaching is done in the classroom, in the lab, online, and in the general operation of the institution. The business community will gravitate toward the more efficient method of communicating and operation. It will require new skills from employees and graduates.

Beyond what is easy to foresee are new programs and offerings that neither community colleges nor universities are predicting now. It will take constant research into what directions quantum computing will lead our society and country in the future. All that is to say, it is incumbent upon administrators and faculty to become aware of the development of quantum computing, follow it carefully through continual research, and be prepared to make appropriate changes in the offerings of the institution for the benefit of students, the business community, and regional economic development.

ADVICE TO STUDENTS

Working and living in the twenty-first century with quantum computing as a reality in the day-to-day world requires that each student be aware of what is coming, when it may affect them, and how they can benefit from it successfully. It would be wise to read about or take an introductory course in quantum computing to get an understanding of this technology, as it will most likely become a part of almost any profession or job in the future. Classical computing in the future will be about as important as cursive handwriting is today. It is critical to learn about what is coming and how to take advantage of it.

Think about the farmer in the early twentieth century who found he could not make a decent living on a farm. He heard about factories in the cities, learned about them, and ultimately sold his farm and moved his family to the city. His work, lifestyle, interests, and successes changed tremendously. He might have become an apprentice and increased his ability and worth to the company he joined. He might have listened carefully to those around him and learned the tricks of the trade, again to increase his capabilities and worth to the company. He might have tried starting his own small business. In other words, he made every effort to become a success in the new environment.

Quantum computing is one path to success in the future. To ignore it would be harmful; to embrace it could bring great success. Extremely rapid communication will create a new environment for employment and living. It is important that the student become ready to move from one job to another by continuously learning. The ability to evolve quickly will become the hallmark of the worker and professional of the future. Quantum computing is an opportunity to be thoroughly investigated.

CONCLUSION

Quantum computing is just one of many technologies currently developing in the twenty-first century. It will offer tremendous possibilities to the business community, health-care organizations, the military establishment, and economic development, to name a few. It will require a workforce with new skills, a growth mentality, and an acceptance of continuous change. Rapid evolution will become the name of the game. Education and training, unlearning and relearning, and reeducation and retraining will become as common as the sunrise and sunset.

CHAPTER SUMMARY

- Today's computers use silicon chips that have doubled in power every eighteen months according to Moore's Law.
- The first transistor was developed in 1957. By 2018, the equivalent of 30 billion transistors could be placed on a chip the size of a fingernail.
- Quantum computing does not use silicon chips; it uses atoms.
- Using atoms takes place in the quantum world, where Newton's laws do not exist.
- Quantum computers use quantum bits, or "qubits," which are exceedingly faster than silicon chips.
- Atoms can be in two places at once, which allows for phenomenal increases in processing speed.
- Working with atoms demands extremely low temperatures at almost absolute zero, some 273 degrees below zero Fahrenheit.
- IBM has a quantum computer that uses qubits in the extremely cold environment required.
- The United States is very interested in developing quantum computing, as is China.

- China is constructing a four-million-square-foot facility at a cost of $10 billion specifically for quantum research.
- Almost thirty universities in the United States have active courses and/or programs in quantum computing.
- The Defense Advanced Research Projects Agency, (DARPA) encourages and provides financial support through grants to develop quantum computing in the United States.
- D-Wave is a Canadian company that developed a quantum computer using magnets.
- China launched the first quantum satellite in 2016 to send encrypted messages from 310 miles out in space using a beam of photons.
- Developing fully operational quantum computers is estimated to take about ten years.
- It is important that higher education administrators be interested in following up with research on the development of quantum computing.
- New courses and programs are in the offing for higher education institutions.
- The classical computer in the future will be about as important as cursive handwriting is today.
- Compare the farmer of the early twentieth century leaving his farm for a job in a factory in the city to the graduate in the twenty-first century moving from using a classical computer to becoming competent with quantum computing.
- Quantum computing is one path to the future. To ignore it could be harmful; to embrace it could bring great success.

REFERENCES

Irving, M. (May 18, 2017). *IBM reveals prototype of its first commercial quantum computer processor*. New Atlas. Retrieved from https://newatlas.com/ibm-next-processor/49590.

Irving M. (May 9, 2017). Nanoscale refrigerator helps quantum computers keep their cool. New Atlas. Retrieved from newatlas.com/nanofridge-cools-quantum-computers/49430.

Jeffery, C. (August 18, 2016). China launches world's first quantum satellite. Retrieved from newatlas.com/china-quantum-cryptography-communication.

Jeffery, C. (May 5, 2016). *IBM brings quantum computing to the masses*. New Atlas. Retrieved from newatlas.com/quantum-processor-qubits-ibm-cloud/43180.

Smith, F. (March 7, 2016). *Quantum computer developed by MIT ushers in a new era of encryption*. EdTech: Focus on Higher Education. Retrieved from edtechmagazine.com/higher/article/2016/quantum-computer.

Timmer, J. (July 7, 2018). D-Wave's quantum computer successfully models a quantum system. Retrieved from arstechnica.com/science/2018/07/d-wave-quantum-computer.

Woodford, C. (December 5, 2018). *Quantum computing*. Explain That Stuff. Retrieved from www.explainthatstuff.com.

Chapter Eleven

Future Technology Centers

Cameron Jackson and Don Miller

Most institutions of higher education in the United States, and subsequently most graduates of U.S. colleges and universities, are not prepared for the science and technology jobs of the future. The Pew Research Center estimates that the United States ranks an unimpressive 38th out of 71 countries in math and 24th in science (DeSilver, 2017). U.S. higher education in the twenty-first century must respond to industry demands for innovative and technology-savvy students with a global perspective.

Dr. Jack O'Daly is the director of research at the Joint Department of Biomedical Engineering, a collaboration between the University of North Carolina and North Carolina State University. According to O'Daly (2018), the United States is not adequately preparing students in the fields of science and engineering. Further, there are not enough high-quality science and engineering programs in the United States (J. O'Daly, personal communication, August 9, 2018).

According to Dr. Matt Meyer, associate VP of education innovations at the North Carolina Community College System, colleges and universities have a responsibility to prepare students for the future by equipping them with employable skills focused on future technologies (personal communication, March 13, 2018). Mike Hogan, associate dean of STEM at Central Piedmont Community College (CPCC) in Charlotte, North Carolina, asserts that colleges and universities must respond to local, regional, and state industry and marketplace demands for a workforce competent in technological processes and systems (M. Hogan, personal communication, June 6, 2018).

Future technologies such as Artificial Intelligence, virtual reality, additive manufacturing, nanotechnology, and quantum computing have amazing implications for the success of virtually every industry around the globe (M. Hogan, personal communication, June 6, 2018). Passionate and visionary higher education leaders must allocate resources toward research and development of programs and facilities needed to prepare students for the future, meet industry demands, and support a strong national economy.

Kacey Grantham (2018), vice president of operations at the tech-savvy global customer acquisition giant Red Ventures, asserts that not only does the company chief executive officer, Ric Elias, expect graduates to come with future-focused perspectives, but that leadership is extremely important to maintain an industry lead in proprietary technologies (K. Grantham, personal communication, March 28, 2018).

BUSINESS AND TECHNOLOGY

Red Ventures

Red Ventures maintains a leading edge in the industry through innovative design and development, and digital marketing and technology strategies. This is done with a very young workforce made up of recent college graduates (K. Grantham, personal communication, March 28, 2018). Recent graduates come from a select handful of top schools capable of preparing students to succeed in such a technology-driven industry (K. Grantham, personal communication, March 28, 2018).

The company is only one of many globally competitive American firms that demand a technologically savvy and future-minded workforce. Apple, Facebook, the U.S. military, and the banking industry are just a few examples of institutions expecting U.S. higher education to meet the demand for a future technology-focused workforce.

Sentient Technologies, Inc.

As another example, the Sentient Technologies, Inc., office in San Francisco, California, depends on a workforce of scientists to work with the company's Artificial Intelligence system who can scour billions of pieces of data, spot trends, adapt as it learns, and make money trading stocks. However, if the Pew Research Center estimates are correct, the science and technology programs at America's top schools are not effectively meeting the demands of American industry or positioning the United States to be globally competitive in the areas of science and technology (DeSilver, 2017).

EXISTING FUTURE-FOCUSED PROGRAMS AND FACILITIES

The spectrum of schools that do offer future-focused technology centers is wide, ranging from regional community colleges to lesser-known small private universities, large public institutes, and globally renowned Ivy League universities. These schools have paved the way and offer a variety of examples for how other schools can develop world-class science and technology programs and facilities. The challenge is twofold, involving leadership and funding. Here are a few examples of U.S. schools that are leading the way:

Joint Department of Biomedical Engineering (BME)

According to O'Daly (2018), the BME is a state-of-the art facility jointly operated by the University of North Carolina (UNC) at Chapel Hill School of Medicine and the North Carolina (NC) State University College of Engineering (personal communication, August 9, 2018). Students, clinicians, and faculty engage in research and technology transfer in areas including biomedical microdevices, medical imaging, pharmaco-engineering, rehabilitation engineering, and regenerative medicine.

"The Joint Department capitalizes on its transformative inter-institutional model by translating discoveries from the academic laboratory setting to the commercial marketplace. BME faculty and students have started 31 companies—and filed 138 patents and 366 invention disclosures" (UNC, "Biomedical Engineering," n.d.). The UNC Chapel Hill endowment was $3 billion at the end of 2017 (UNC, "Annual Report," n.d.). The NC State endowment was $1.23 billion as of October 2017 (NCSU, "Foundations Accounting and Investments," n.d.).

According to O'Daly, higher education leadership with a vision to develop a future-focused program such as biomedical engineering should consider the following recommendations:

> The optimal facility for future-focused biomedical engineering programs would be of significant size; at least 50–60,000 square feet of varied and flexible space. This space would be at least 65% laboratory space, with the remaining 35% of the space serving as offices, large and small meeting rooms, and storage. The laboratory space would be of a varied nature commensurate with the broad range of the biomedical engineering discipline. For instance, laboratories will be needed to serve engineering intensive areas such as rehabilitation and medical devices; instrument intensive areas such as imaging; and biologically intensive areas such as pharmacoengineering and regenerative medicine. A facility as described above will cost at least $50 million. (J. O'Daly, personal communication, August 9, 2018)

Costs Involved

O'Daly describes the equipment, technology, and associated costs for a new facility as significant. Typical costs of these pieces of equipment may include the following:

    Ultrasound Imagers: $50,000 each
    Biological Safety Cabinets: $15,000 each
    Dual Strip Treadmills: $100,000 each
    Virtual Reality Display: $500,000
    Motion Capture System: $50,000
    Chemical Fume Hoods: $20,000 each
    Incubators: $1,500 each
    Autoclaves: $20,000 each
    High-Performance Workstations and Storage: $20,000
    3D Printers: $15,000 each
    CNC Milling Machine: $100,000 (J. O'Daly, personal communication, August 9, 2018).

The price tag for new high-tech facilities and associated equipment, as outlined above, can be daunting and simply not financially feasible for most colleges and universities. However, colleges and universities with strong leadership, creative partnerships, and solid financial grounding should be contributing to a stronger U.S. national economy and preparing current and future students for high-tech jobs of the future. Here are several other examples of U.S. institutions with world-renowned future-focused high-tech facilities. Industry partnerships, well-funded endowments, and visionary leadership are a common thread.

Cornell NanoScale Science and Technology Facility (CNF)

The CNF at Cornell University in Ithaca, New York, supports a wide variety of nanoscale science projects, including the study of cell-sized robots and other microelectromechanical devices, advanced materials processing, and biotechnology devices (Fleischman, 2018). This state-of-the-art facility is supported by the National Science Foundation, Empire State Development's Division of Science, Technology, and Innovation (NYSTAR), industry partners, the university, and over eight hundred facility users (50% non-university) per year (Fleischman, 2018). Cornell is a large private university with over 23,000 students and an endowment of $6.8 billion as of 2017 (Cornell, n.d.).

The Southern Institute of Manufacturing and Technology (SiMT)

According to Mark Roth, executive vice president at Florence-Darlington Community College, the SiMT is an agile and configurable 143,000-square-foot future technologies center at Florence-Darlington Technical College in Florence, South Carolina (personal communication, February 14, 2018). The SiMT includes the largest 3D prototyping tools and materials available in the Southeast and provides products and services through the co-located Additive Manufacturing Center (AMC) (M. Roth, personal communication, February 14, 2018).

The facility supports student learning and salable high-tech solutions such as additive manufacturing, a 3D interactive production studio, large-scale 3D printing, Social Media Listening, and rapid prototyping tools and materials to industry (M. Roth, personal communication, February 14, 2018). The SiMT facility also includes an Advanced Machining Center to develop advanced manufacturing processes and automated manufacturing techniques and has an interactive production studio where students and industry customers use virtual training simulators for medical sciences and manufacturing training scenarios (M. Roth, personal communication, February 14, 2018).

Virtual reality training in criminal justice and surgical technologies reduces the risk of injury to students. The additive manufacturing center allows companies to develop prototypes and test them before they go on the market. The facility is funded both by state funds, industry partners, the college, and facility users (M. Roth, personal communication, February 14, 2018).

CalTech Center for Autonomous Systems and Technologies (CAST)

The CalTech Center for Autonomous Systems and Technologies (CAST) supports students, academic researchers, and industry through interdisciplinary research and an exchange of ideas surrounding autonomous systems (CalTech, 2018). Research at CAST includes but is not limited to drones and robots for use in science, industry, and medicine.

Students and other researchers address issues of sensing, control, vision, and other emerging technology areas. CAST is an incubator for translating student and faculty ideas into reality (CalTech, 2018). CAST is supported by CalTech, government, industry, and other users. CalTech is a small private university with only 2,300 students and 300 faculty, but it has produced an astounding thirty-two Nobel laureates (CalTech, 2018). CalTech's endowment is $2.6 billion as of 2017 (CalTech, 2018).

The Center for Machine Learning Design and Intelligence Laboratory (DILAB)

The Center for Machine Learning DILAB at Georgia Institute of Technology in Atlanta, Georgia, teaches students Knowledge-Based Artificial Intelligence (KBAI). Machine learning is a subcategory of Artificial Intelligence using algorithms that enable computers to learn and react, hypothesize, and make predictions and decisions (Becker, 2018). Georgia Institute of Technology established the Center for Machine Learning in June 2016 and offers a Ph.D. in machine learning to "train the next generation of leaders" (Becker, 2018, p. 1).

Georgia Tech is home to the Advanced Technology Development Center (ATDC), which has supported entrepreneurs launching more than 170 tech companies since 1980, with 90 percent of those tech startups succeeding after five years; those companies have generated over $12 billion in Georgia (ATDC, 2018). Georgia Tech is a public school ranked in the top-ten colleges and universities in America, with 29,000-plus students and an endowment of $1.6 billion at the end of 2017 (Georgia Tech, 2018).

The Advanced Technology Center (ATC)

The new ATC at Central Piedmont Community College is an 85,000-square-foot, five-story facility completed in June 2018, at a cost of $25 million (C. Paynter, personal communication, June 6, 2018). According to Mike Hogan, associate dean for STEM at CPCC, the facility consists of advanced manufacturing labs and classrooms to serve as the home base for multiple technology-driven student learning and corporate partner support programs, including mechatronics, electrical and mechanical engineering, the engineering transfer program, and others that serve advanced manufacturers and logistics, energy, and STEM-related employers in Charlotte, North Carolina (M. Hogan, personal communication, June 6, 2018).

According to Chris Paynter, dean of STEM at CPCC, the ATC will not only prepare students for careers in emerging technologies, but also serve corporate partners and hundreds of employers by helping future advanced technology-driven manufacturing grow in Mecklenburg County, North Carolina, and the surrounding region (C. Paynter, personal communication, June 6, 2018).

Other examples of world-renowned programs in the United States include the Stanford Genome Technology Center, which is only a short drive to large tech companies such as Apple, Google, and Facebook, all of whom recruit heavily from Stanford (Stanford University, n.d.); the Carnegie Mellon Center for Technology Transfer and Enterprise Creations; Georgia Institute of Technology; Massachusetts Institute of Technology; and the Princeton Plasma Physics Lab.

There are common threads among each of these examples of future-focused programs and facilities. The first is visionary higher education leadership. Leaders must be willing to take a risk with industry partners to develop programs and build facilities for emerging technologies and markets.

According to Hogan (2018), future-focused facilities must be easily adaptable to changing technologies, with modular equipment, rather than fixed, when possible, in order to keep long-term facility and renovation costs down. Hogan (2018) also stated that future-focused ventures are more likely to succeed when industry partners vested in maintaining a competitive leading edge are involved and are supportive of expensive technology-focused higher education projects (M. Hogan, personal communication, June 6, 2018).

FUTURE TECHNOLOGIES AND FUTURE-FOCUSED ENGINEERING PROGRAMS

Future technologies such as Artificial Intelligence, virtual reality, additive manufacturing, nanotechnology, and quantum computing have amazing implications for how community colleges and universities operate. Not only should educational institutions be thinking about how these technologies could make their own processes more efficient; they should also be looking for ways to partner with local industry to train the workforce of the future.

According to O'Daly (2018), the UNC/NC Joint Biomedical Engineering program partners with numerous existing industries and businesses to develop and sustain the program, including companies such as Seimens, Novo Nordisk, Galaxo-Smith-Kline (GSK), Agilent, Beckton-Dickenson (BD), FujiFilm, Biogen, Imaging Instrumentation manufacturers, Pharma, and other industries including medical devices, prosthetics, and diagnostics (J. O'Daly, personal communication, August 9, 2018).

The price tags for future-focused programs and facilities can make them seem cost prohibitive. However, partnerships with industries can tip the scales to create a viable opportunity for more institutions of higher education to engage in future-focused programs. O'Daly (2018) has said that programs should "promote entrepreneurial activity and provide sufficient infrastructure and autonomy to encourage creative team-based project development" (J. O'Daly, personal communication, August 9, 2018).

Additionally, future technologies can help community colleges and universities make internal processes more efficient. After implementing Artificial Intelligence to control the sprinkler system at University of Texas–Austin, the program coordinator for irrigation and water conservation saved the institution $1,000,000 last year (Gardner, 2018).

According to Gardner (2018), Artificial Intelligence is "quietly, but inexorably, transforming college campuses" (p. B4). The advising department at Georgia State University has partnered with AdminHub to offer automated texts to students that provide advising (Gardner, 2018). In the summer of 2016, the system answered more than 200,000 questions from Georgia State students (Gardner, 2018).

While the coordinator at University of Texas is excited about the technological advances his department has made, he also realizes that continuing to use Artificial Intelligence will require a more tech-savvy staff (Gardner, 2018). "There's going to be a skills gap that we're all worried about," said Don Guckert, facilities manager at the University of Iowa (as cited in Gardner, 2018, p. B7).

It is apparent that in some areas, like manufacturing, the skills gap is already here. According to a 2015 study done by consulting firm Deloitte, between 2015 and 2025, 3.5 million manufacturing jobs will need to be available, but there will only be 1.5 million workers who are skilled enough to fill these positions (Giffi, 2015).

COMMUNITY COLLEGES

This is where community colleges and universities can come in: to fill that gap through the expansion of existing programs and the creation of new ones. While a Google CEO recently said that Artificial Intelligence could do more for humanity than fire or electricity, some worry about a loss of privacy (AI-Spy, 2018).

As Artificial Intelligence becomes more ubiquitous in the workplace, workers will need more training. For instance, "Slack, a workplace messaging app, helps managers assess how quickly employees accomplish tasks" (AI-Spy, 2018, p.15). Since more scrutiny will be put on productivity, workers need better training. As Amazon discusses the possibility of delivering packages thirty minutes after orders through the use of drones (Gardner, 2018), colleges and universities recognize the need to train workers who can operate this relatively new technology.

According to Gose (2018), at "a growing number of institutions around the country, degree programs that teach students how to operate drones are multiplying" (p. B10). Along with package delivery, other uses of drones could be crop health assessments, aerial photography to make home listings more attractive, and bridge and pipeline inspection (Gose, 2018). According to a drone trade group, drones could "contribute $82 billion to the U.S. economy in the decade ending in 2025" (Gose, 2018, p. B11).

Virtual Reality

Virtual reality has incredible implications for the classroom. At SiMT at Florence-Darlington Community College, Basic Law Enforcement Training (BLET) students can virtually learn how to disarm hostile attackers without putting themselves at risk. Surgery technology students can enter a virtual surgery theater, aiding surgeons without any risk to a real patient. According to Evans (2018), other implications of virtual reality include an accounting class using a virtual reality restaurant owner simulator or an art professor leading his students through an exhibit at a Paris museum.

A literature professor might lead his students down the jazz-infused streets of New York City in the 1930s, exposing them to the vibrancy of the Harlem Renaissance. However, virtual reality "is still impeded by expensive hardware, health concerns, and a lack of training for faculty members" (Evans, 2018, p. B18). Again, community colleges and universities can step in to meet this training need by creating new programs and expanding existing ones.

While there are several established Artificial Intelligence programs at universities, there are few at community colleges. Most universities offer Artificial Intelligence classes within their computer science departments, but few offer Artificial Intelligence majors. Palomar College is one of the only community colleges with an Artificial Intelligence presence. The college has partnered with AI Solutions to create the "AI Project." The project includes a robot that walks around campus and engages with students (Palomar College, 2017).

Santa Monica College

Another part of the AI project is strategically placed tablets that can help students find buildings on campus (Palomar College, 2017). Santa Monica College is another community college that has an Artificial Intelligence program. A $385,000 grant from the United Negro College Fund helped the institution to expand the program (Santa Monica College, 2017). Universities that have notable Artificial Intelligence programs include Carnegie Mellon, MIT, Stanford, and the University of California–Berkeley.

Carnegie Mellon has an Artificial Intelligence major and boasts such accomplishments as "pioneering innovations in intelligent digital libraries, data representations and algorithms, market clearing technologies, and complex task-embedded robotic applications" (Carnegie Mellon, n.d.).

It has now become quite common for universities to have 3D printers in their libraries. These printers can be used by students and faculty for a fee. Colleges that specialize in STEM, like Virginia Tech, the University of Michigan, and Penn State, have laboratories, in which there is more than one 3D printer. Schools like LSU and Texas A&M have even bigger facilities. Very few community colleges have 3D printing.

Somerset Community College

An example is Somerset Community College, which boasts Kentucky's first certificate in 3D printing (Somerset Community College, n.d.). Through a grant, local businesses can experiment with 3D printing for free (Somerset Community

College, n.d.). Somerset has worked with biomedical companies and Hearthside Foods in London, Kentucky (Somerset Community College, n.d.).

Unlike most community colleges, Somerset has several 3D printers in its classrooms (Somerset Community College, n.d.). Somerset has partnered with local businesses like Dremel Tool and has been able to expand the program through grant money (Somerset Community College, n.d.). Program coordinator Eric Wooldridge articulated the benefits of additive manufacturing:

> Once we get the opportunity to show local businesses how this technology can help their bottom line and production, they are excited to integrate it into their factories and offices. Giving them access to a quality printer helps get them off and running so they can incorporate 3D printing in numerous aspects of their operations. (E. Wooldridge, personal communication, June 4, 2018)

The model of creating partnerships with local industry and securing funding through grant money seems to be a good one for any small to midsize institution that wants to start an additive manufacturing program. Wooldridge believes that while universities can produce the engineers that oversee additive manufacturing facilities, community colleges can train the workers who have to actually run the machines (E. Wooldrige, personal communication, June 4, 2018).

Robotics programs are far more common at community colleges than other future technologies. One key to the success of these programs is partnerships with industry. For example, Ivy Tech Community College in Indianapolis partners with Subaru, Honda, and Caterpillar (Ivy Tech Community College, 2018).

Calhoun Community College

Calhoun Community College in Alabama partners with many industries, including Kawasaki Robotics, Mitsubishi Electric, and SAS automation (Alabama Robotics Technology Park, 2016). Calhoun Community College is one of the community colleges in Alabama that partners with the state, the universities, and the robotics industry to operate the Robotics Technology Park, located in Tanner (Alabama Robotics Technology Park, 2016).

The $73 million park includes three large facilities that serve industry needs (Alabama Robotics Technology Park, 2016). The Robotics Maintenance Training Center is a 60,000-square-foot facility that houses free training for Alabama industries that wish to automate. The Advanced Research and Development Center includes four client suites provided for industry partners; the Integration, Entrepreneurial, and Paint Dispense Training Center provides training and/or space for manufacturing process integration (Alabama Robotics Technology Park, 2016).

Indian River State College

Indian River State College in Florida has a twenty-one-month Robotics and Photonics Institute (Indian River State College, n.d.). The college offers internships with local companies for students in the institute (Indian River State College, n.d.). Classes are held at the Knight Center for Emerging Technologies, which is a $20 million facility that "houses two virtual studios with green screen technology. . . . Network security and web development are the focus in the Cyber Security Institute, and the Advanced Manufacturing Suite and Photonics Laboratory create a unique environment for study of robotics and light and laser technologies" (Indian River State College, n.d.).

Universities that have prominent robotics programs include Carnegie-Mellon, which features the 100,000-square-foot National Robotics Center (Carnegie-Mellon University, n.d.), The University of Minnesota, Georgia Tech, and Florida State.

Few community colleges have nanotechnology programs. Some that do include Forsyth Technical Community College in North Carolina, Northern Virginia Community College, and Chippewa Valley Technical College (CVTC) in Wisconsin.

Northern Virginia Community College

The program at Northern Virginia Community College was established in 2015. A nanoscience classroom at Northern Virginia Community College includes "desktop scanning electron microscopes, atomic force microscopes, and 3D optical profilers" (Northern Virginia Community College, 2015). CVTC has a 38,000-square-foot applied-technology center that has a nanoscience laboratory and state-of-the-art machine tool equipment (CVTC, 2018). CVTC partners with economic development agencies, Wisconsin universities, and industries (Chippewa Valley Technical College, 2018).

Universities that have nanotechnology programs include the University of Pennsylvania, Michigan Tech, the University of Washington, and Purdue University. Purdue's 186,000-square-foot Discovery Park includes a 25,000-square-foot nanotechnology laboratory (Purdue University, 2018). Purdue leases a nanotechnology incubator lab to interested companies (Purdue University, 2018).

BENEFITS TO BUSINESS AND INDUSTRY

According to the Charlotte Chamber of Commerce, advanced manufacturing is one of the targeted industries for future employment (Charlotte Chamber, 2017). Some of the companies that have manufacturing headquarters in the Charlotte area include Ingersoll Rand, Coca-Cola, Electrolux, Corning, and

Husqvarna (Charlotte Chamber, 2017). There is a great need for training of employees in advanced manufacturing. In many of the companies listed above, the development of prototypes would be useful.

According to Martin, Bowden, and Merrill (2014), "Additive manufacturing has become a breakthrough for companies that specialize in the design of new products by allowing rapid-prototyping" (p. 31). A school in the Charlotte area should definitely pursue a major in which students can learn additive manufacturing. While some community colleges like Wake Technical Community College offer certificates in additive manufacturing, universities like Penn State and the University of Maryland offer master's degrees in the subject, Penn State's program being completely online.

A school would need to weigh its available resources to decide whether an undergraduate certificate or a graduate degree would be more appropriate. "Terry Wohlers, principal consultant and president at Wohlers Associates, Inc., said less than 1% of practicing engineers and designers that need to understand additive manufacturing have the right knowledge and skills" (Guillot, 2017, May 3).

It is a safe bet that there are some employees of Charlotte companies that would benefit from training in additive manufacturing. UNC–Charlotte, N.C., A&T, and N.C. State are currently researching additive manufacturing through a UNC general administration grant (University of North Carolina at Charlotte, 2017). Another school in North Carolina would be advised to enter into this partnership or to start research into beginning an additive manufacturing program immediately to not fall behind the competition.

Training in robotics would also be helpful to Charlotte industries. North Carolina schools like Vance-Granville Community College, Cleveland Community College, and Central Piedmont Community College have robotics programs. At UNC–Charlotte, students can choose an AI, Robotics, and Gaming Concentration within a Computer Science major, but there is no major in Robotics. Only two robotics courses are offered. It would appear that there are promising opportunities for other schools in North Carolina to tap into a largely unexplored market.

THE PRODUCTION OF SALABLE PRODUCTS

Certainly, there are many possibilities for future technology programs to produce salable products through the use of additive manufacturing. Wooldridge indicated that the aerospace and automobile industries will be using more and more parts that can be produced through additive manufacturing (personal communication, June 5, 2018). As examples, Wooldridge pointed to parts for seat belts in cars and engine parts for Caterpillar tractors (E. Wooldridge, personal communication, June 5, 2018).

According to Guillot (2017), "3D printed parts are now being used in everything from shoes to airplanes and rocket engines being used by NASA." Wooldridge emphasized that the printing materials were more important than the actual printer (E. Wooldridge, personal communication, June 5, 2018). The program at Somerset Community College started with a low-cost Maker-Bot printer, then expanded to printers made by Ludbot and Mark II (E. Wooldridge, personal communication, June 5, 2018). The program now uses industrial-grade printers, which typically cost more than $5000.

SiMT has produced a simulation model for a shut-down nuclear power plant that facilitated a quick repair and prototypes for wearable virtual reality equipment (SiMT, 2018). SiMT also provides virtual reality services for Fortune 500 companies (SiMT, 2018). Services have included virtual welding and forklift operations (SiMT, 2018). SiMT also offers virtual training for law enforcement offices and surgical technicians (SiMT, 2018).

OUTLOOK

Short Term (1–5 Years)

Community colleges and universities have a responsibility to find ways to better educate students in future technologies like additive manufacturing, robotics, artificial technology, and nanotechnology. According to the Pew Research Center, the United States is already behind in STEM areas (DeSilver, 2017). The country will continue to fall behind if colleges do not make a larger investment in future technologies.

Mid-Term (5–10 Years)

Visionary college leaders will see an opportunity for their institutions; there are clear gaps between the number of future technology jobs and the number of trained workers (Giffi, 2015). While universities can equip engineers to run factories, community colleges can train workers to run the machines. Partnerships between community colleges and universities are needed.

Long Term (10–20 Years)

Schools with successful future technology programs partner with businesses, showing them the benefit of future technologies to their bottom lines. While future technology centers are expensive, they can help close the gap between future technology jobs and equipped workers. Universities, community colleges, and by extension, boards of trustees and state legislatures will need to make a financial commitment to training workers in these emerging technologies if the United States is to remain competitive with other countries.

CONCLUSION

Future technology centers are the bridge to the digital future that will be accepted and used by business and industry. Community colleges and universities will need to adapt to the changes in terms of programs, equipment, and facilities. It is critical that higher education work shoulder-to-shoulder with the technology developments that will drive business and industry in the future. Future-focused institutions will be able to support the employment needs of the future with ease while others may flounder in attempts to catch up. The digital future is here.

CHAPTER SUMMARY

- Most institutions of higher education are not prepared for the technology jobs of the future.
- Future technologies have amazing implications for industries.
- Red Ventures is an industry that maintains a leading edge in the use and design of digital technology strategies.
- The spectrum of schools that offer future-focused technology centers is wide, ranging from community colleges to universities.
- Costs for developing a future-focused technology center is considerable.
- In order to meet those costs, institutions of higher education may need to partner with business and industry.
- Federal grants can also be of great help in developing future-focused technology programs.
- The SiMT includes the largest 3D prototyping tools and materials available in the Southeast.
- The SiMT supports virtual reality training in criminal justice and the surgical technologies.
- The Center for Machine Learning at Georgia Institute of Technology in Atlanta, Georgia, teaches students knowledge-based Artificial Intelligence.
- The Advanced Technology Center at Central Piedmont Community College in Charlotte, North Carolina, provides training in megatronics, electrical and mechanical engineering, the engineering transfer program, and others that serve advanced manufacturers and STEM-related employers.
- Future technologies such as Artificial Intelligence, virtual reality, additive manufacturing, nanotechnology, and quantum computing have amazing implications for how community colleges and universities will operate.
- It is apparent in some areas, like manufacturing, that a skills gap already exists.
- As Artificial Intelligence becomes more ubiquitous in the workplace, workers will need more training.

- Virtual reality has incredible implications for the classroom.
- There are several established Artificial Intelligence programs at universities; however, there are few at community colleges.
- Santa Monica College has an Artificial Intelligence program funded by a $385,000 grant from the United Negro College Fund.
- Carnegie Mellon has an Artificial Intelligence major.
- Somerset Community College in Kentucky has a certificate in 3D printing.
- Robotics programs are far more common at community colleges than other future-focused technologies.
- Calhoun Community College in Alabama operates the robotics technology park.
- Indian River State College in Florida has a twenty-one-month Robotic and Photonics Institute.
- Very few community colleges have nanotechnology programs.
- Universities with nanotechnology programs include the University of Pennsylvania, Michigan Tech, the University of Washington, and Purdue University.
- According to the Charlotte Chamber of Commerce, advanced manufacturing is one of the targeted industries for future employment in the area.
- There are many possibilities for future technology programs to produce salable products through the use of additive manufacturing.
- In the next five years, community colleges and universities have a responsibility to find ways to better educate students in future technologies.
- In the long run, schools with successful future technology programs will have partnered with businesses showing them the benefit of future technologies to their bottom lines.
- Future technology centers are the bridge to the digital future that will be accepted and used by business and industry.

REFERENCES

Advanced Technology Development Center. (2018). Startup Success, Engineered. Retrieved from https://www.atdc.org/about/.

AI-Spy: The workplace of the future. (2018, March 28). *The Economist.* Retrieved from https://www.economist.com/leaders/2018/03/28/the-workplace-of-the-future.

Alabama Robotics Technology Park. (2016). *Our partners.* Retrieved from https://alabamartp.org/.

Becker, T. (2018, March 8). *The minds of the new machines: New theories and innovative algorithms support computer learning for improved prediction and decision making.* Retrieved from https://www.rh.gatech.edu/features/minds-new-machines.

CalTech. (2018). *CalTech at a glance.* Retrieved from https://www.caltech.edu/content/caltech-glance.

Carnegie Mellon University. (n.d). *Artificial intelligence.* Retrieved from https://www.csd.cs.cmu.edu/research-areas/artificial-intelligence.

Carnegie Mellon University. (n.d.). Center for Technology Transfer and Enterprise Creations. Retrieved from https://www.cmu.edu/cttec/industry/index.html.

Charlotte Chamber. (2017). *Targeted industries.* Retrieved from https://charlottechamber.com/eco-dev/targeted-industries/.

Chippewa Valley Technical College. (2018). *Manufacturing Education Center.* Retrieved from https://www.cvtc.edu/experience-cvtc/campuses/manufacturing-education-center.

Cornell University. (n.d.). *University Facts.* Retrieved from https://cornell.edu/about/facts/cfm.

DeSilver, D. (2017, February). U.S. students' academic achievement still lags that of their peers in many other countries. *The Pew Research Center.* Retrieved from http://www.pewresearch.org/fact-tank/2017/02/15/u-s-students-internationally-math-science/.

Evans, A. (2018, April 13). Virtual reality can enable real learning. *The Chronicle of Higher Education,* pp. B17–18.

Fleischman, T. (2018, January, 2). Physicists take first step toward cell-sized robots. *Cornell Chronicle.* Retrieved from http://www.cnf.cornell.edu/doc/2018cnfNM_v27n1.pdf.

Gardner, L. (2018, April 13). Artificial intelligence makes its way into every corner of the campus. *Chronicle of Higher Education,* pp. B4–B7.

Georgia Tech. (2018). *Academic Excellence.* Retrieved from https://www.gatech.edu./about/rankings.

Giffi, C. (2015). The skills gap in U.S. manufacturing. *Deloitte.* Retrieved from https://www2.deloitte.com/us/en/pages/manufacturing/articles/boiling-point-the-skills-gap-in-us-manufacturing.html.

Gose, B. (2018, April 13). Drone degree programs take flight. *Chronicle of Higher Education.* pp. B10–B11.

Guillot, C. (2017, August 29). How manufacturers can get the most out of 3D printing. *Chief Executive.* Retrieved from https://chiefexecutive.net/how-manufacturers-can-get-the-most-out-of-3d-printing/.

Guillot, C. (2017, May 3). More universities are offering degrees in additive manufacturing. *Chief Executive.* Retrieved from https://chiefexecutive.net/universities-offering-degrees-additive-manufacturing/.

Indian River State College. (n.d.). *Robotics and photonics institute.* Retrieved from https://www.irsc.edu/programs/advancedtechnology/RoboticsPhotonics/roboticsphotonics.aspx?id=4294972753.

Ivy Tech Community College. (2018). *Advanced automation and robotics technology.* Retrieved from https://www.ivytech.edu/advanced-automation-robotics/.

Martin, R. L., Bowden, N. S., & Merrill, C. (2014). 3D printing in technology and engineering education. *Technology and Engineering Teacher, 73*(8), 30–35.

Northern Virginia Community College. (2015, February 17). *Nanoscience classroom installed at Northern Virginia Community College.* Retrieved from https://www.prweb.com/releases/2015/02/prweb12530195.htm.

North Carolina State University. (n.d.). *Foundations Accounting and Investments.* Retrieved from https://projects.ncsu.edu/project/fdns-acct/endowment_fund/UnivEnd_FY2017Perf.pdf.

Palomar College. (2017). *Artificial intelligence project.* Retrieved from https://www2.palomar.edu/pages/artificialintelligence/.

Purdue University (2018). *Discovery Park.* Retrieved from https://www.purdue.edu/discoverypark/.

Santa Monica College. (2017). *Robotics & artificial intelligence at SMC: The wave of the future.* Retrieved from http://www.smc.edu/NewsRoom/Pages/Robotics-Artificial-Intelligence.aspx.

Somerset Community College. (n.d.). *SCC 3D printing program helps local businesses incorporate additive manufacturing through partnership with Dremel tool and grant funds.* Retrieved from Somerset Community College website: https://somerset.kctcs.edu/news/10262017_scc_3d_printing_prog_helps_local_busi_incorp_additive_manuf_thru_partnership_with_dremel_tool_and_grant_funds.aspx.

Southeastern Institute of Manufacturing and Technology. (2018). *An interactive production studio success story.* Retrieved from https://simt.com.cgi-bin/p/awtp-custom.

Stanford University (n.d.). *Genome Technology Center.* Retrieved from http://med.stanford.edu/sgtc/.

University of North Carolina–Chapel Hill. (n.d.). *Annual Report.* Retrieved from https://uncmc.unc.edu/files/2017/09/CHIF-FY2017-AnnualReport.pdf.

University of North Carolina–Chapel Hill. (n.d.). *Biomedical Engineering*. Retrieved from https://www.bme.unc.edu/about/.

University of North Carolina–Charlotte. (2017, August 3). *Inside UNC-Charlotte*. Retrieved from https://inside.uncc.edu/news-features/2018-02-25/unc-charlotte-remembers-its-longtime-champion-irwin.

Epilogue

Understanding technology in the twenty-first century is extremely critical to the success of community college and university leaders. Assuming that life goes on in a linear manner will become a notion lost in the past. The exponential development of technologies and the businesses and industries they affect will create a world far different from anything that is currently known.

Those involved in higher education as administrators and faculty will need to be well educated in the direction and speed that the technologies will take. Administrators and faculty cannot be caught off-guard; they will need to know how various technologies will impact their respective institutions. Once that is known, actions can be taken to make certain that community colleges and universities can remain viable and useful in the future.

Hopefully this book, which provides a baseline for where the technologies are in the late second decade of the twenty-first century, will be of considerable assistance to those in higher education who are trying to make sense of the changes they will soon encounter. Changes they will have to deal with in terms of courses, programs, and even the mission of the institutions themselves. What is known as normal today will in a matter of years become something close to ancient history. It is critical that all those in education are able to deal with what is to come. If not, the technologies will deal with them.

About the Editor

Darrel W. Staat hails from Michigan, where he received his doctorate in English from the University of Michigan, his master's degree in English from Western Michigan University, and his bachelor's degree with a major in English from Hope College, located in Holland, Michigan.

Since 2015, he has held the position of coordinator and assistant professor of the Community College Executive Leadership Program (CCEL) at Wingate University in Wingate, North Carolina. He teaches six graduate courses and administers the CCEL program. During 2014, he taught online courses at the undergraduate and graduate levels.

In October 2013, he retired from the position of president of the South Carolina Technical College System in Columbia, South Carolina, a position he held for over three years. Previously he served as the president of Central Virginia Community College in Lynchburg, Virginia, for eleven years.

Before that, he served for five years as the founding president of York County Community College in Wells, Maine, and four years as the president of Eastern Maine Community College in Bangor, Maine. While president of those various institutions, he was highly involved in local economic development and community affairs, serving in leadership positions on a considerable number of local boards.

As a mid-administrator, he spent thirteen years at Florence-Darlington Technical College in Florence, South Carolina, and four years at Northeastern Technical College in Cheraw, South Carolina. He also taught courses at Coker College, Francis Marion University, and Limestone College in South Carolina. As a faculty member, he spent four years at Southwestern Michigan College in Dowagiac, Michigan. He began his career teaching seventh and eighth grades at Jenison Junior High in Jenison, Michigan.

About the Contributors

Sylvia Cox holds a master's degree in language and literacy and an EdS in community college administration. She is currently the vice president of student services at Southeastern Community College in Whiteville, North Carolina.

Kira Ferris holds a master's degree in the science of anthropology and an EdS in community college administration. She is currently completing graduate work at Wingate University (Ballantyne Campus) in Charlotte, North Carolina.

Ghada Gouda holds a master's degree in education-international management and policy and an EdS in community college administration. She is currently a faculty member at ECPI in Charlotte, North Carolina.

Cameron Jackson holds a master's degree in public administration and an EdS in community college administration. He is currently the assistant vice president for auxiliary services at Wingate University in Wingate, North Carolina.

Nita Johnson holds a master's degree in public relations organizational communications and an EdS in community college administration. She is currently an adjunct faculty member at Central Piedmont Community College in Charlotte, North Carolina.

Dahmon King holds a master's degree of business administration in technology management and an EdS in community college administration. He is currently the program director for industrial and engineering technologies at York Technical College in Rock Hill, South Carolina.

Angelo Markantonakis holds a master's degree in education and an EdS in community college administration. He is currently the associate vice president of academic affairs at Rowan-Cabarrus Community College in Salisbury, North Carolina.

Don Miller holds a master's degree in fine arts: creative writing, a master's degree in English, and an EdS in community college administration. He is currently an associate professor of English at Guilford Technical Community College in Jamestown, North Carolina.

Melissa Price holds a master's degree of arts and an EdS in community college administration. She is currently the director of dual enrollment K–12 programs at Midlands Technical College in Columbia, South Carolina.

Mark Roth holds a master's degree in business administration and an EdS in community college administration. He is currently the executive vice president at Florence-Darlington Technical College in Florence, South Carolina.

Renata Sims holds a master's degree in public administration and an EdS in community college administration. She is currently a faculty member at York Technical College in Rock Hill, South Carolina.

www.ingramcontent.com/pod-product-compliance
Lightning Source LLC
Chambersburg PA
CBHW022013300426
44117CB00005B/169